A RAINBOW OF AFGHANS

A RAINBOW OF AFGHANS

by Leslie Linsley

Photographs by Jon Aron

Sedgewood® Press New York

For Sedgewood® Press:

Director: *Elizabeth P. Rice*
Project Manager: *Connie Schrader*
Project Editor: *Sydne Matus*
Production Manager: *Bill Rose*
Cover & Graphic Design: *Jos. Trautwein / Bentwood Studio*

Craft Contributors:

Photographs on pages 57, 80, 151 courtesy of Bernat Yarns &
    Craft Corp.

Photograph on page 165 courtesy of Phildar, Inc.

Diagrams: Robby Smith
Color illustrations: Peter Peluso, Jr.

Acknowledgments:

I would like to extend my appreciation to the yarn manufac-
turers and distributors who have been helpful in the prepa-
ration of this book. Their cooperation and interest in this
project has been most generous. They are:
Bernat Yarn and Craft Corp., Uxbridge, Massachusetts
Brunswick Worsted Mills Inc., Pickens, South Carolina
Crystal Palace Yarns, Berkeley, California
Lane Borgosesia, USA, Ltd., North Salem, New York
Phentex USA, Inc., Plattsburgh, New York
Phildar Inc., Norcross, Georgia
Tahki Imports Ltd., Moonachie, New Jersey
William Unger & Co., Inc., New York, New York

Dedicated to the many wonderful crafters
who have done so much to keep needlework
alive in this country.
The tradition of American needlework
is part of the heritage of future generations.

Dear Crafter:

We are delighted that you have in your hands *A Rainbow of Afghans.* You'll see more than seventy color combinations in full color in the pages of this book— enough to give you quite a choice! Each photograph is accompanied by one or two other color combination samples, rendered in artwork, enabling you to see at a glance how one pattern will look worked in different colors.

This book is one of many published to date by Sedgewood® Press (and we have many more planned for the future). Sedgewood, begun in 1982, exists in order to bring you high-quality books with fine designs, both traditional and unusual uses for projects, clear instructions, and full color throughout, with every project shown in a color photograph.

Proud as we may be of our books, though, the real proof of their success is in the doing. We hope you will enjoy *A Rainbow of Afghans,* will use it happily to create your own personal afghans, and will look forward to the publication of more Sedgewood titles.

Sincerely,

Elizabeth P. Rice
Director, Sedgewood® Press

CONTENTS

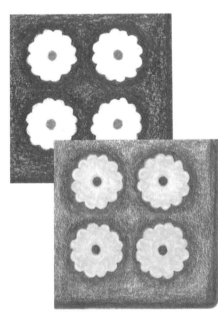

Introduction

Everyone loves afghans. Whether it's a traditional granny-square crochet or an overall white Aran knit, anyone who knows how to knit or crochet wants to make an afghan. Perhaps it's because, when finished, the project is useful, good-looking, and of lasting value. I've written several books on knit and crochet. The projects have been diversified, ranging from quick-and-easy items to sell at bazaars to afghans that take longer to make. The most popular projects are always the afghans.

There never seem to be enough patterns to choose from. Sometimes we want to make something quickly. Other times we like to have projects to work on a little at a time while relaxing in front of television. Everyone seems to like carry-along projects to work on in spare moments.

I receive many letters from readers. The most often asked question is whether a certain afghan can be made in another color. The person may like the pattern, but be insecure about changing the color of the yarn. Since it takes a commitment of time, effort, and money, most of us want to be sure that we will like the results. If we can't see the finished project in our choice of colors, we're not sure how it will look if the originals are changed.

I thought it would be a good idea to present a book of knit and crocheted afghans in a variety of colors for each of them. Some of the afghans can be made in a weekend, such as the Easy Lap Throw on page 90. There are also some very special afghans such as Spring Garden on page 61 to give as a wedding gift, and afghans to make in pieces for carrying with you, such as the Daisy Crib Cover on page 75. There are also afghans for all situations: some for babies, some as lap throws, and others to fit beds.

The results, presented here, offer a variety of patterns and styles and have been designed in combinations of pleasing colors. However, alternative colors are suggested for each afghan. In this way you have a choice for your finished projects. For example, a warm-colored afghan can easily be made with a cool-color combination for those who live in a warm climate or want a summer cover. One person might want to make an afghan to use as a lap throw in the den. Another person might like the same pattern, but want to make the afghan in colors more suited to the bedroom. To help you envision a change of color, many of the afghans on the following pages are accompanied by a color sketch showing an alternative set of yarn colors that can be used. You will see the colors in relation to one another before you begin the work.

I've also included complete information about the yarns used for each afghan. For example, each list of materials will tell you the name of the manufacturer, the type of yarn used (such as knitting or worsted weight), and the yardage or weight of each skein. In this way, if you can't find the exact yarn shown here, you'll be able to substitute a similar yarn to get the same look and size.

And finally, I've tried to present a nice combination of knits and crochets that are interesting, but not terribly difficult to do. I know that we're all busy with other activities and the experience of making an afghan should be enjoyable and free of frustration. There are two or three projects that are aimed at the more advanced needleworker, but not so difficult that a beginner can't tackle them. The Fluffy Baby afghan on page 47 and the Textured Knit on page 108 are examples of these.

I hope you'll enjoy this collection of designer afghans. Perhaps you'll come up with some novel color combinations of your own.

LESLIE LINSLEY

Knitting Basics

LEARNING TO KNIT

Knitting is based on learning how to do two basic stitches, knit and purl. From these you can make all kinds of knitted projects. By combining these two stitches in different variations, such as 2 knit, 2 purl, or 1 row of knit and 1 row of purl, you will be able to create a simple garment or as elaborate a project as you can imagine.

As a beginner, you will find that most of the projects in this book confine themselves to a basic knit and purl stitch to produce what is known as a stockinette pattern. This is the most popular stitch combination and is easy to learn. If you are a practiced knitter, you'll find a variety of projects that introduce new ideas and combinations of yarn that will make them enjoyable to do. Best of all, the projects are quick and easy, but the results should be rewardingly professional-looking.

The following will teach you what you need to know in order to make the knitting projects in this book. You will also be able to go on to create your own designs or variations on the original patterns.

CASTING ON

To begin any project, you will need to cast a specified number of stitches onto your needles. This becomes the base on which you will work your first row of knitting. When counting rows, do not count the cast-on row.

1. (Refer to figure 1.) Start by making a slip knot, leaving a tail of yarn about 3 inches long. Place the loop of the knot on the left-hand needle. (Left-handers should reverse these and all other instructions.) Use your right-hand needle to make the stitches to cast onto the left-hand needle as follows.

2. Wrap the yarn around your right ring finger to create tension, and insert the right-hand needle from front to back through the loop on the left-hand needle. The two needles are now in the loop, with the right-hand needle behind the left.

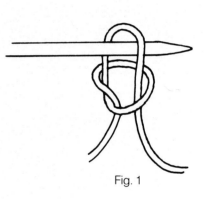

Fig. 1

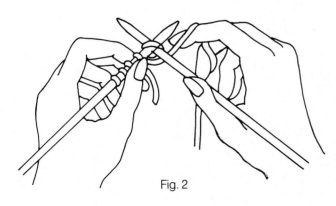

Fig. 2

3. (Refer to figure 2.) Bring the yarn clockwise around the right-hand needle. With the right-hand needle, pull the yarn through the loop on the left needle.

4. Bring the tip of the left-hand needle from right to left through the loop on the right needle.

5. Withdraw the right-hand needle, pull the yarn slightly taut, and you have 2 stitches on the left needle (figure 3). Continue to do this until you have the required number of stitches.

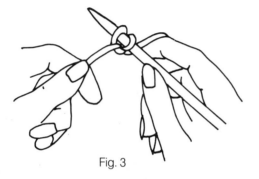

Fig. 3

KNIT STITCH

A project worked with all knitting stitches, every row knit, is called a garter-stitch fabric.

1. Hold the needle with cast-on stitches in your left hand, with the yarn around your left forefinger. Insert the right-hand needle from front to back through the first loop on the left-hand needle as shown in figure 1.

KNIT

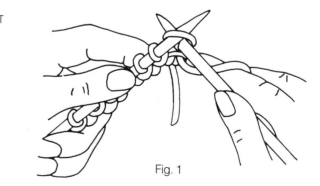

Fig. 1

2. Bring the yarn under and over the point of the right needle (figure 2). Draw the yarn through the loop with the point of the needle (figure 3).

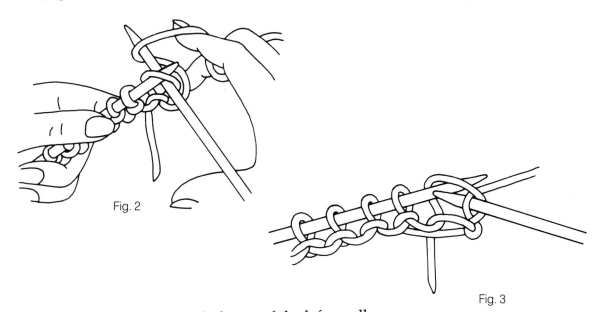

Fig. 2

Fig. 3

3. Use your right forefinger to push the tip of the left needle down to let the loop on the left needle slip off. You now have 1 stitch on your right needle (figure 4). Work across the row in this way.

Fig. 4

After finishing a row of knitting, transfer the right-hand needle to left hand and the left-hand needle to the right hand, turning the needles also (the points always face each other), and continue the next row in the same way, always taking the stitches from the left to the right needle.

When you have practiced making nice neat rows at an even tension, you can turn this garter stitch into a project.

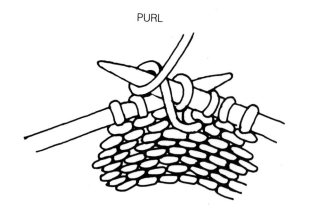

PURL

Fig. 1

PURL STITCH

1. With cast-on stitches on your left-hand needle, insert the point of your right-hand needle from right to left through the front of the first stitch. With the yarn in front of your work (rather than in back as with the knit stitch), wind it over and around the needle's point. (See figure 1.)

2. Draw the yarn back through the stitch and let the loop on the left needle slip off the needle. Your first purl stitch is now on your right-hand needle.

STOCKINETTE STITCH

Work 1 row with the knit stitch. Purl each stitch in the next row. Continue to knit 1 row and purl the next row for a stockinette fabric. The pattern on the front of the work is that of interlocking V's. The back of the fabric looks like a tighter version of the garter stitch (knit every row).

INCREASING A STITCH

This means that you will be making 2 stitches from 1. Knit the first stitch as usual, but do not drop the stitch off the left-hand needle. Bring the right-hand needle behind the left needle and insert it from right to left into the back of the same stitch. Make another stitch by winding yarn under and over the right-hand needle (knit stitch). Slip the stitch off the left-hand needle. (See figure 2.)

Fig. 2

DECREASING A STITCH

If you are decreasing stitches, to shape a raglan armhole, for example, you will be knitting or purling 2 stitches together to form 1 stitch. In a pattern the direction will be given as k 2 tog or p 2 tog. (See figure 3.)

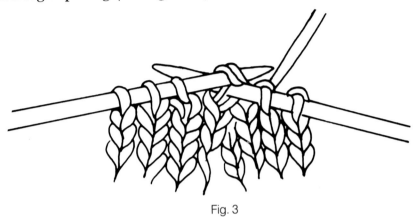

Fig. 3

On the right side of your work, knit 2 stitches together as if they were 1. If worked through the front of the stitches, the decrease slants to the right; if through the back of the stitches, it slants to the left.

When decreasing a purl stitch, work on the back side and purl 2 stitches together.

Psso means pass slip stitch over and is another way of decreasing a stitch. You slip the first stitch (as if to knit) onto the right-hand needle from the left without knitting it, keeping the yarn in back of the work. Knit the next stitch and bring the slip stitch over the knit stitch as you would when binding off (see below). (When slipping a stitch in a purl row, keep the yarn in front of the work.)

BINDING OFF

1. Knit the first 2 stitches. Insert the left-hand needle from left to the right through the front of the first (the right-most) stitch (figure 1).

BINDING OFF

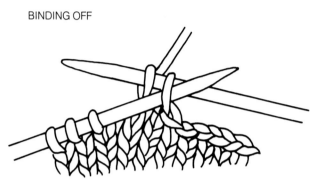

Fig. 1

2. (Refer to figure 2.) Lift the first stitch over the second stitch and the tip of the right-hand needle. (Use your left hand to push the tip of the right-hand needle back while pulling the stitch through.) Let the lifted stitch drop, and you now have 1 stitch on the right-hand needle. (See figure 3.) Knit another stitch and lift the right-most stitch over the next as before. Repeat this across the row until 1 stitch is left.

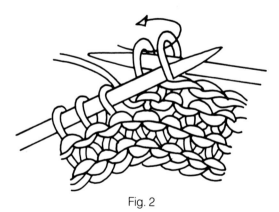

Fig. 2

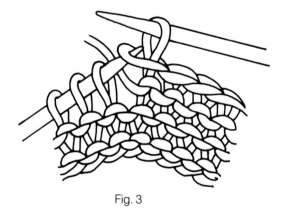

Fig. 3

3. Loosen the remaining loop on the right-hand needle and withdraw the needle. Cut the yarn, leaving 2 or 3 inches (unless the instructions for your project specify a longer tail), and pull this tail through the loop. (See figure 4.) Tighten the knot.

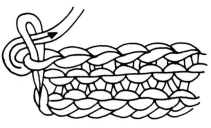

Fig. 4

CABLE STITCHES

Cable stitches are often used in fisherman knit and to add interest to a plain project.

Producing a cable twist requires the use of a double-pointed cable needle. This should be the same size or slightly smaller than the needles used to knit the afghan.

Determine where the cable will be and begin on the right side of the work. Knit or purl as per project directions until you come to the point where the cable will begin. Insert one end of the cable needle from right to left through the next stitch. Allow this stitch to slip off the left-hand needle (reverse for left-handed people). Repeat for the next two stitches. Keep the cable needle with the three stitches on it at the front of the work. Ignoring this needle, take the yarn to the back of the work and knit the next three stitches with the other two needles as usual.

Next, hold the cable needle with your left hand and push the stitches to the right side of the needle. Using the right-hand needle, knit the three stitches on the cable needle. Purl to the end of the row. Work the straight rows between cable twists according to the directions for each project. Always twist your cable on the right side of your work. The cable will have tighter or looser twists depending on the number of rows between twists. The fewer the rows between twists, the tighter the cable pattern.

JOINING NEW YARN

Always join new yarn at the beginning of a row. If you get partway across and run out of yarn, pull out stitches to the beginning of the row and add the new yarn. (This is to avoid knots in the middle of a piece.) Insert the right-hand needle into the first stitch on the left-hand needle. Wrap the new yarn around the right-hand needle, leaving a tail as you did when you started your work. Pull the right-hand needle through the first stitch and continue to knit as before. Pull the side strands of yarn to tighten. Use these to attach pieces of the project being worked, or weave them into the project later.

KNITTING TIPS
Yarn

There are hundreds of yarns to choose from, and each has its best uses. Most projects recommend the best yarn. If the brand name is not given, the yarn group usually is. This might be bulky weight, worsted, sport yarn, etc. If you are substituting yarns for those given in a project, be sure that the weight is similar. Look for a yarn with the same gauge. This information is usually found on the label of the yarn.

Often the yarn looks quite different when it is made up from what it looked like on the skein. It's a good idea, especially when using expensive yarn or when making a large project, to buy only one skein and make a swatch. In this way you can see what the knitted yarn will look like before making the investment of time and money. Then buy enough yarn of the same dye lot needed for a project. Often colors change from one dye lot to another, and you may have trouble matching yarns later on if you run out.

Gauge

The gauge is the number of stitches per inch and the number of rows per inch that you knit with the yarn and needles recommended. The gauge is the tension at which you work, and this determines the size of the project. This is especially important when making a garment to wear. If your gauge doesn't match the gauge given with the pattern, the garment won't fit as expected to.

Before beginning any project, test your gauge by making a swatch using the yarn and needles recommended. Knit a 4 × 4-inch square in the specified stitch pattern. Check the gauge as follows: If the gauge calls for 7 stitches to 2 inches, for example, count 7 stitches in the middle of the work and insert pins where they begin and end. With a tape measure check to see what the measurement is for 7 stitches. If the 7 stitches make less than 2 inches, your gauge is too tight. Make another sample with needles a size larger. If the 7 stitches measure more than 2 inches, you will need to go down a size with your needles. Check the gauge for rows as well as for stitches. Sometimes a gauge difference occurs because the yarn used is not exactly what is recommended.

BLOCKING

Many of the afghans require blocking after they are finished. This means squaring them off to the correct size and shape.

Different yarns must be treated differently, and this is why it's important to keep the labels from your yarn to refer to after the knitting has been completed. Sometimes the label gives blocking directions, but if not, you will need the information concerning what the yarn is made of.

When making a granny-square afghan, for example, you want each piece to have the correct shape. If you've worked in a stockinette stitch, the edges tend to curl and blocking is necessary. Each piece must be pinned down and pressed. The iron setting depends on the yarn. Use a cool iron on synthetic material, but natural fibers can be pressed with a warm iron. Some blocking is done by placing a damp cloth over the shaped and pinned piece. Press over the damp cloth and remove it. Then wait until the piece is dry before removing the pins. It is not advisable to press over a garter-stitch fabric.

ASSEMBLING PIECES

There are many ways to assemble pieces of a project that must be stitched together. Some projects here recommend leaving enough of a tail of the yarn being used to sew pieces together.

Main seams are usually joined with a backstitch. With right sides of fabric together, use a blunt yarn needle to make small stitches across the material just below the finished edges.

To join sections of ribbing, use an overcast stitch. With right sides together and edges matching, overcast the yarn on both pieces. Do not pull the yarn too taut; keep it loose for a flat seam.

Another way to join seams, especially for bulky yarn, is with a slip-stitch crochet.

DUPLICATE STITCH

This stitch is used on top of knitting stitches. Use a contrasting yarn color, and thread it through a tapestry or embroidery needle. Working from the wrong side of the afghan, bring the needle through the center of the lower point of the stitch. Insert the needle at the top right-hand side of the same stitch. Bring the needle horizontally through the yarn in back of the stitch, to the top left side of the stitch. Insert the needle into the base of the same stitch. You will have completely covered the stitch being worked over.

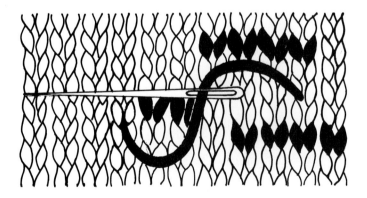

SEED STITCH

On the first row *K1, P1, repeat from * to end of row. On all subsequent rows, K over the P st and P over the K st.

KNITTING ABBREVIATIONS

beg — beginning

CC — contrasting color

CR — cable right

dec — decrease

dp — double-pointed knitting needle

inc — increase

k — knit

LC — left cable

LH — left-hand needle

lp — loop

MC — main color

p — purl

pat — pattern

psso — pass slip stitch over

RC — right cable

rem — remaining

rep — repeat

RH — right-hand needle

rnd — round

sk — skip

sl — slip

sl st — slip stitch

st — stitch

St st — stockinette st

sts — stitches

tog — together

wyib — with yarn in back

wyif — with yarn in front

yo — yarn over needle

* — repeat what comes after

(   ) — work directions in parentheses as
many times as specified. For example: (1k, 3p) 3 times.

CROCHET BASICS

CHAIN STITCH

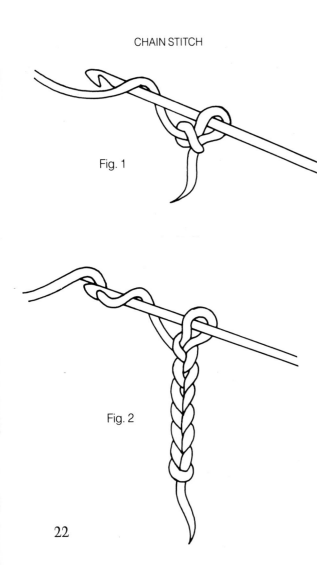

Fig. 1

Fig. 2

LEARNING TO CROCHET

Most of the crocheted projects can be made with a few basic stitches. All the work starts with a chain made up of a series of loops on a crochet hook. Unlike knitting, which is done on two, three, and sometimes four needles, crocheting is done on a single hook. Hooks come in various sizes. The size you use will depend on the yarn, pattern, and project.

Most yarn used for knitting can also be used for crocheting. However, very fine crochet cotton is best for the fine lacy items made with crochet stitches rather than by knitting.

CHAIN STITCH

All projects here begin with the chain stitch.
1. Make a slip knot by taking yarn about 2 inches from the end and winding it once around your middle three fingers.

2. Pull a length of yarn through the loop around your fingers. Put this new loop on your crochet hook and pull tight.

3. With yarn wound over left-hand fingers, pass the hook under the yarn on your index finger and catch a strand with the hook (figure 1).

4. Draw the yarn through the loop already on the hook to make 1 chain stitch (figure 2). Repeat steps 3 and 4 for as many chain stitches as needed. If you hold the chain as close to the hook as possible with the thumb and index finger of your left hand, the chain will be even.

SINGLE CROCHET

The beginning of every project in crochet is a row of a specific number of chain stitches. These are the basis of the piece, just as the cast-on row is the basis of a knit piece.

At the beginning of every row, an extra chain stitch is made. This is counted as the first stitch of the row and is called the turning chain.

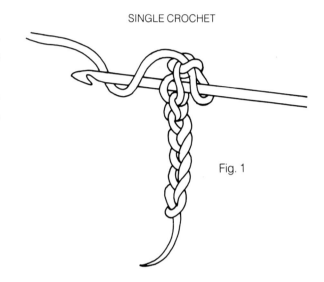

Fig. 1

1. After making the initial chain, insert the hook in the 2nd chain from the hook (the skipped chain is the turning chain) and bring the yarn over the hook from back to front (clockwise) (figure 1). Pull the yarn over through the chain so you have 2 loops on the hook, as shown in figure 2. (Note that in these instructions, each chain stitch is simply called a chain. When a string of chain stitches is being discussed, it is known by the number of stitches—for example, "first ch 5" means the first group of 5 chain stitches in a row.)

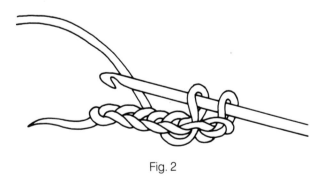

Fig. 2

2. Wind the yarn around the hook again and draw the hook with its 3rd loop through the 2 loops already on the hook. You have made 1 single crochet (sc).

23

3. Continue to work a single crochet in each chain stitch (figure 3). At the end of the row, make 1 chain (ch 1) and turn your work around from right to left so the reverse side is facing you.

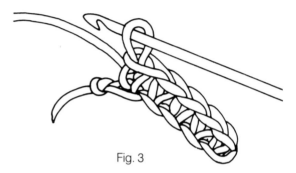

Fig. 3

4. The turning chain stitch counts as the first stitch. Work the next single crochet by inserting your hook through the 2 top loops of the next stitch in the previous row. Wind the yarn over the hook (yo) and draw it through the stitch. Wind the yarn over again and pull it through the two loops on the hook. Continue to work a single crochet in each stitch across the row. Chain 1 and turn.

FASTENING OFF

At the end of all required rows or rounds, cut the yarn with a tail of 2 or 3 inches and draw it through the last loop at the end of the row. Pull tightly and weave it out into the fabric with a yarn needle. Sometimes the tail is used to sew pieces together. If this is the case, leave a tail that is long enough.

DOUBLE CROCHET

1. With your foundation chain made, bring yarn over hook and insert hook under top loops of 4th chain from hook.

2. (Figure 1) Yarn over hook. Draw through chain. There are 3 loops on hook.

3. (Figure 2) Yarn over hook. Draw through 2 loops on hook. There are now 2 loops on hook.

4. (Figure 3) Yarn over hook. Draw yarn through the last 2 loops on hook. One double crochet (dc) is completed (figure 4). Insert hook into next stitch in foundation chain and repeat steps 2, 3, and 4.

Once you've worked a double crochet in every chain across the row, ch 3 and turn. This turning chain of 3 chain stitches counts as 1 double crochet beginning the next row.

5. Skip first stitch and work double crochet in top 2 loops of each double crochet across.

6. Work double crochet in first stitch of ch 3 (turning chain).

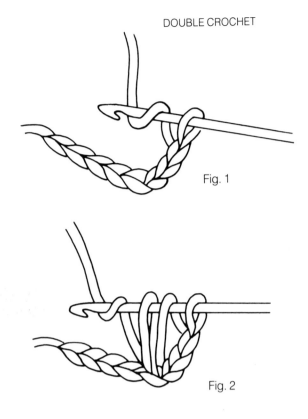

Fig. 1

Fig. 2

Fig. 3

Fig. 4

HALF DOUBLE CROCHET

Make a foundation chain.

1. Yarn over hook and insert hook through loop of 3rd chain from hook (figure 1).

2. (Figure 1) Yarn over hook. Draw yarn through the chain so there are 3 loops on hook (figure 2).

3. (Figure 3) Yarn over hook. Draw through all 3 loops to complete half double crochet (hdc) (figure 4).

Continue to do this in each chain across row. At end of row, ch 2 to turn. Skip first stitch and work first half double crochet into each half double crochet across. Last hdc in row is worked in turning ch. Ch 2 to turn.

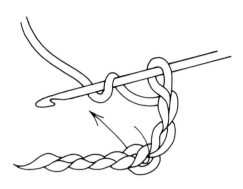

Fig. 1

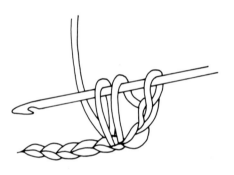

Fig. 2

Fig. 3

Fig. 4

TREBLE OR TRIPLE CROCHET

Make a foundation chain.

1. With 1 loop on your hook, put the yarn over the hook twice (figure 1).

2. Insert hook in 5th chain from the hook, yarn over hook, and pull loop through chain, making 4 loops on hook.

3. Yarn over, draw through 2 loops at once (figure 2). There are now 3 loops on hook.

4. Yarn over and pull through 2 loops (figure 3). There are now 2 loops on hook.

5. Yarn over and pull through last 2 loops (figure 4), completing 1 triple crochet (tr).

6. At end of row, ch 4 and turn. This turning chain of 4 is the first triple crochet of the next row (figure 5).

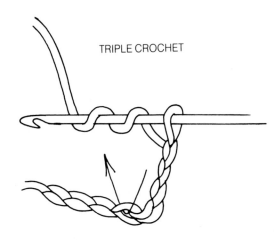

TRIPLE CROCHET

Fig. 1

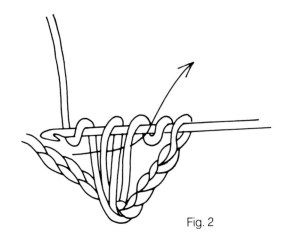

Fig. 2

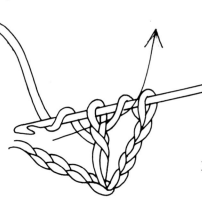

Fig. 3

Fig. 4

Fig. 5

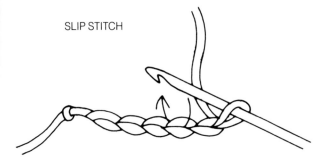

SLIP STITCH

Fig. 1

Fig. 2

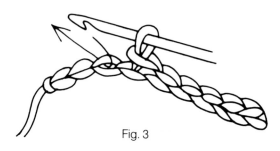

Fig. 3

TURNING

You will need a number of chain stitches at the end of each row to bring your work into position for the next row. The number of chain stitches depends on the crochet stitch you are working. For single crochet, you will ch 1 to turn; for half double crochet, you will ch 2; for double crochet, you will ch 3; and for treble or triple crochet, ch 4.

SLIP STITCH

Insert hook into chain (figure 1). Yarn over hook and draw through both stitch and loop on hook in one motion (figure 2). This completes 1 slip stitch (sl st). A slip stitch is used to join a chain in order to form a ring (figure 3). Insert hook through 2nd top strand of stitch. Yarn over hook and draw through stitch and loop on hook in one motion.

WORKING IN SPACES

In crochet work that is lacy and contains openwork, often a stitch in the preceding row is skipped; instead, you will be instructed to chain across the gap. Sometimes your pattern tells you to work stitches in a space instead of in a stitch. In that case, insert your hook through the gap or space (sp) rather than through a stitch in the preceding row. Often several stitches are worked in one space, as a way of increasing stitches.

INCREASING SINGLE CROCHET

When a pattern calls for an increase of a single crochet, work 2 stitches in 1 stitch (figure 1).

DECREASING SINGLE CROCHET

When a pattern calls for a decrease of a single crochet, pull up a loop in 1 stitch, then pull up a loop in the next stitch so there are 3 loops on your hook (figure 1). Yarn over hook and draw through all 3 loops at once (figure 2).

INCREASE SINGLE CROCHET

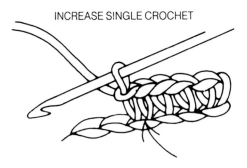

Fig. 1

DECREASE SINGLE CROCHET

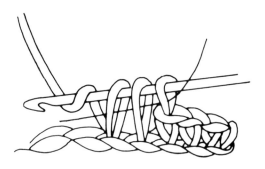

Fig. 1

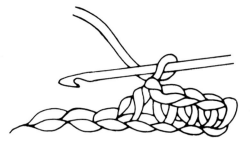

Fig. 2

CROCHETING TIPS
Yarn

Most yarn used for knitting can also be used for crocheting. However, very fine crochet cotton will enable you to achieve a more delicate lacy motif than is possible with traditional knitting yarns.

As with knitting, it is best to buy all the yarn you need to finish a project at one time, from the same dye lot. Often the colors change slightly from one dye lot to another, and if you run out in the middle of a project, you may not find the exact yarn you need to finish.

Gauge

Make a swatch approximately 4 × 4 inches using the yarn, hook, and stitch pattern recommended. This will give you a chance to see the yarn made up as well as to check the gauge before beginning the project. Count the number of stitches that should equal the given inches and mark with pins at beginning and end. With a tape measure on the flat swatch, check to see if they correspond. If you have fewer stitches per inch than the pattern calls for, your work is too loose. Change to a smaller hook. If you have more stitches per inch than you should, go up one hook size. Make another swatch to be sure the gauge is correct, and adjust accordingly. Check the gauge for rows as well as for stitches.

AFGHAN STITCH

Row 1: Draw up a loop in each st of ch, leaving all loops on hook as shown in figure 1. Take loops off as follows: Yarn over hook, draw through 1 loop, *yo, draw through 2 loops, repeat from * across the row as shown in figure 2. The loop remaining on hook counts as the first loop of the next row. (See figure 3.)

Row 2: Skip the first upright bar and draw up a loop in the next and each remaining upright bar, leaving all loops on the hook. Take loops off in the same way as Row 1. Repeat only Row 2 for desired length (figure 4).

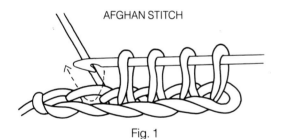

AFGHAN STITCH

Fig. 1

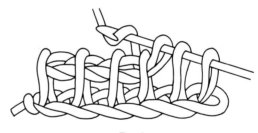

Fig. 2

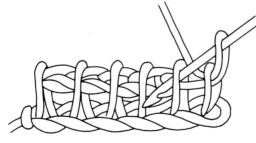

Fig. 3

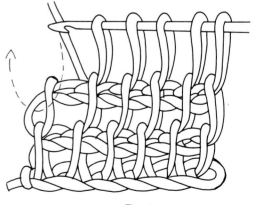

Fig. 4

CROCHET ABBREVIATIONS

beg — beginning

bet — between

ch — chain

cl — cluster

dc — double crochet

dec — decrease

grp — group

hdc — half double crochet

inc — increase

L — left

lp — loop

pat — pattern

R — right

rem — remaining

rep — repeat

rnd — round

sc — single crochet

sk — skip

sl st — slip stitch

sp — space

st — stitch

tog — together

tr — treble or triple crochet

yo — yarn over hook

* — repeat what comes after

( ) — work directions in parentheses as many times as specified.

For example: (dc 1, ch 1) 3 times.

CROSS-STITCH OVER AFGHAN STITCH

Each upright bar across the row of an afghan st is counted as 1 st. When a cross-stitch design is indicated for a project, you will be provided with a chart. Follow the chart and count upright bars. There are 2 holes formed by the afghan st *after* each upright bar.

Working from left to right, join color on wrong side at the lower hole and work across next upright bar to upper hole. Then bring the needle through the lower hole directly below as shown in figure 5. Continue on number of sts for color being used. Then work from right to left to form cross. Do not pull yarn too tight.

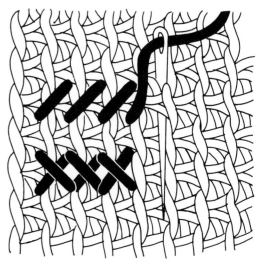

Fig. 5
CROSS-STITCH OVER
AFGHAN STITCH

BASIC EMBROIDERY STITCHES

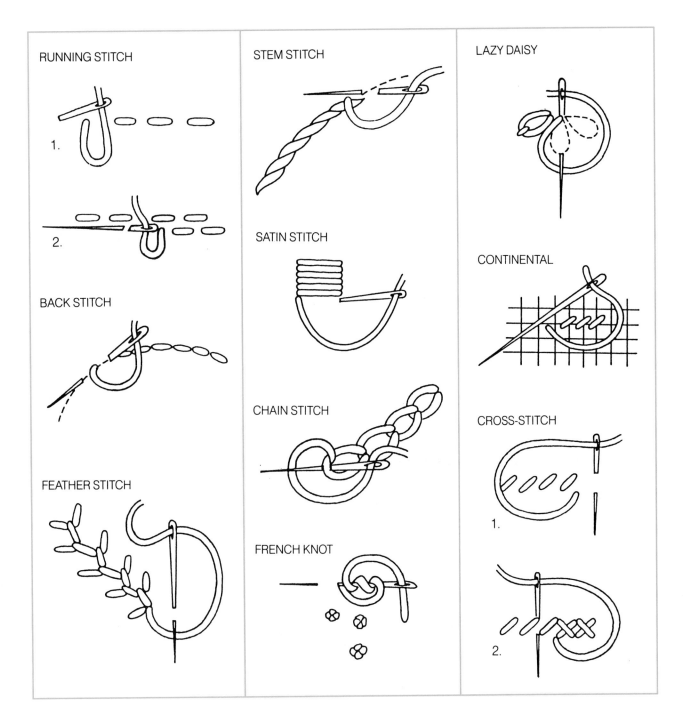

RUNNING STITCH

1.

2.

BACK STITCH

FEATHER STITCH

STEM STITCH

SATIN STITCH

CHAIN STITCH

FRENCH KNOT

LAZY DAISY

CONTINENTAL

CROSS-STITCH

1.

2.

Patchwork

A *traditional quilting pattern is used to knit this pretty green, blue, and white afghan. As you can see, this color combination creates a warm and homey design, reminiscent of a patchwork quilt. It's a wonderful project for a country home. However, if this color combination doesn't fit into your decorating scheme, you can use the same pattern with a different color combination.*

The 12-inch squares make it easy to finish in no time. It's also perfect for a carry-along project as each square fits easily into your bag. Made from 100% orlon and acrylic 4-ply yarn, it is completely washable. The finished size is 60 × 72 inches.

MATERIALS: Brunswick Windrush (3.5 oz./100 gram skeins)—6 skeins each of color A (blue velvet ombre) and B (deep blue velvet); 5 skeins each of color C (gray) and color D (sea green). **Interchangeable Yarns:** Brunswick Germantown knitting worsted or Heatherblend.

Knitting Needles: #8 (5 mm) or size needle for correct gauge.

Crochet Hook: #6/G (4.5 mm) for trim.

GAUGE: 5 sts = 1 inch; 6 rows = 1 inch.

DIRECTIONS

Make 30 squares, then assemble with 5 squares across and 6 down.

Rows 1 & 2: With color C cast on 56 sts and k 1 row, p 1 row.

Rows 3 through 11 (odd-numbered rows): With color C k 2, with color A seed st (k1, p1) 8, with color B k 36, with color A seed st 8, with color C, k 2.

Rows 4 through 12 (even-numbered rows): With color C p 2, with color A seed st 8, with color B p 36, with A seed st 8, with C p 2.

Rows 13 through 21 (odd-numbered rows): With C k 2, with B k 8, with A seed st 8, with D k 20, with A seed st 8, with B k 8, with C k 2.

Rows 14 through 22 (even-numbered rows): With C p 2, with B p 8, with A seed st 8, with D p 20, with A seed st 8, B p 8, C p 2.

Rows 23 & 25: C k 2, B k 8, D k 8, C k 20, D k 8, C k 2.

Row 24: C p 2, B p 8, D p 8, C p 20, D p 8, B p 8, C p 2.

Rows 26 & 28: C p 2, B p 8, D p 8, C p 3, B p 14, C p 3, D p 8, B p 8, C p 2.

Row 27: C k 2, B k 8, D k 8, C k 3, B k 14, C k 3, D k 8, B k 8, C k 2.

Rows 29 through 37 (odd-numbered rows): C k 2, B k 8, D k 8, C k 3, B k 3, A seed st 8, B k 3, C k 3, D k 8, B k 8, C k 2.

Rows 30 through 38 (even-numbered rows): C p 2, B p 8, D p 8, C p 3, B p 3, A seed st 8, B p 3, C p 3, D p 8, B p 8, C p 2.

Rows 39 & 41: C k 2, B k 8, D k 8, C k 3, B k 14, C k 3, D k 8, B k 8, C k 2.

Row 40: C p 2, B p 8, D p 8, C p 3, B p 14, C p 3, D p 8, B p 8, C p 2.

Rows 42 & 44: C p 2, B p 8, C p 20, D p 8, B p 8, C p 2.

Row 43: C k 2, B k 8, D k 8, C k 20, D k 8, B k 8, C k 2.

Rows 45 through 53 (odd-numbered rows): C k 2, B k 8, A seed st 8, D k 20, A seed st 8, B k 8, C k 2.

Rows 46 through 54 (even-numbered rows): C p 2, B p 8, A seed st 8, D k 20, A seed st 8, B p 8, C p 2.

Rows 55 through 63 (odd-numbered rows): C k 2, A seed st 8, B k 36, A seed st 8, C k 2.

Rows 56 through 64 (even-numbered rows): C p 2, A seed st 8, B p 36, A seed st 8, C p 2.

Row 65: C k 56.

Row 66: C p 56. Bind off.

TO FINISH

Work 1 row sc with A, decreasing as necessary to take in across the top and bottom. Each square should measure 12 inches. With right sides tog and corners matching, use large needle threaded with yarn to catch the *outside loop only* of each st on each square and sew in this manner. Make 5 strips 6 squares long, then sew strips tog. Work 3 rows sc around entire afghan with color A. Make 3 sc in each corner to turn.

VARIATION NO. 1

A – black
B – gray
C – dark green
D – red

VARIATION NO. 2

A – burnt orange
B – forest green
C – ochre
D – brown

Checkerboard

*I*f you want to make a simple knit afghan for baby, this is the one for you. Made with the all-knit garter stitch, each square measures 5 inches. Simply slip the yarn and your needles into your purse for an easy carry-along project. As you can see, the blue and white combination is quite pretty, but any color will work with white. The finished size is 27 × 41 inches, just right for a crib or carriage.

MATERIALS: Knitting worsted weight (3.5 oz./100 gram balls)—3 balls each of color A (white) and color B (blue).

Knitting Needles: #10 (6 mm) or size needed for correct gauge. Yarn needle.

GAUGE: Garter st (all knit) 4 sts = 1 inch; 7 rows = 2 inch. Each square = 5 inches.

DIRECTIONS

Make 18 white squares and 17 blue squares.
Cast on 20 sts. Knit across each row until you have 19 rows. Each square will be approximately 5 × 5 inches. Fasten off.

TO FINISH

Beginning with a white square, then a blue square, arrange the squares so you have alternating colors in 7 rows of 5 squares each. Using one of the yarn colors, sew all together from the wrong side.

Edging: Attach white yarn 2 rows before corner. * Work 6 dc in corner st, skip 2 sts, sl st in next st, skip 2 sts. Repeat around afghan from *.

VARIATION NO. 1

A – pale green
B – pale peach

VARIATION NO. 2

Use equal amounts of red, yellow, and blue. Arrange squares as shown.

Jewel Lap Blanket

*M*ade with Tahki's "Windsor Tweed" and "Superkid Mohair," this deep-colored afghan has a rich and luxurious look. The tweed yarn is a 100% new wool that is mothproof. The mohair is combined with it to make the project soft and fluffy. Both yarns are a dream to work with. They make this afghan quite special because of the variety of unusual colors and textures.

However, while this afghan was made with shades of six colors, it can be made with shades of only two colors for an equally pretty project (see color sketch).

Designed by Karin Strom, the finished project is approximately 42 × 66 inches and is made with a seed stitch.

MATERIALS: Takhi "Windsor Tweed" (3.5 oz./100 gram skeins)—1 skein each of color A (kelly green), B (fuchsia), C (royal blue), D (teal blue), E (plum), F (blue); Tahki "Superkid Mohair" (1.4 oz./40 gram balls)—1 each of color G (green), H (red), I (turquoise), J (plum), K (blue), L (red).

Knitting Needles: #13 (9 mm) 29-inch circular needle or size needed for correct gauge.

GAUGE: Seed st: 3 sts = 1 inch; 4 rows = 1 inch.

DIRECTIONS

Beginning at side edge with A cast on 200 sts.

NOTE: When starting a new series of colors, knit the first row.

Large Stripe

Row 1: *K 1, p 1, rep from * across.

Rows 2 through 6: K the p sts and p the k sts (seed-stitch pattern).

Row 7: With color G, k across.

Row 8: With G, repeat Row 1.

Rows 9 & 10: With G, repeat Rows 2 & 3.

Row 11: With A, k across.

Row 12: With A, repeat Row 1.

Rows 13 through 16: With color A, rep Rows 2 through 5.
Using color B in place of color A, and H in place of color G, rep Rows 1 through 16.
Using color C in place of color A, and I in place of color G, repeat Rows 1 through 16.

Using color D in place of color A, and J in place of G, repeat Rows 1 through 16.
Using E in place of A, and K in place of G, repeat Rows 1 through 16.
Using F in place of A, and L in place of G, repeat Rows 1 through 16.

Small Stripe

Rows 1 through 4: With color A, repeat Rows 1 through 4 of large stripe.

Rows 5 through 8: With color G, repeat Rows 7 through 10 of large stripe.

Rows 9 through 12: With color A, repeat Rows 11 through 14 of large stripe.
Keeping to same color sequence as on large stripe, repeat Rows 1 through 12 for small stripes. Work until the 6th small stripe is completed. Bind off all sts.

TO FINISH

Fringe (Worked along each short edge of the blanket): Cut 5 strands of color A approximately 14 inches long. Fold in half and draw loop end through side edge of the large A and G stripe. Pull the loose ends through the loop and draw tightly.

Work 4 fringes, evenly spaced, along each side edge of A and G stripe. Using color B for fringes along B and H stripe, C for fringes along C and I stripe, D for fringes along D and J stripe, E for fringes along E and K stripe, and F for fringes along F and L stripe, work 4 fringes along each side edge of large stripes.

Keeping to the colors established, work 3 fringes along each side edge of the small stripes. Trim the ends.

VARIATION NO. 1

A, C, E – red
B, D, F – dark green
G, I, K – pink
H, J, L – light green

VARIATION NO. 2

A – medium blue
B – bright green
C – dark blue
D – olive green
E – purple
F – deep green
G, I, K – pale blue
H, J, L – pale green

Fluffy Baby

*B*ee Gonnella used William Unger & Co.'s Fluffy baby yarn to make this seed-stitch baby afghan. It is completely washable, but feels just like mohair to the touch. The soft pink, green, and blue colors combine with a border of white for a delightful gift to give a new mother. It will fit a carriage or bassinet. The finished size is approximately 26 × 28 inches.

This afghan was made with a dominant pink color. The sketch shows you what green and white bands around a yellow afghan might look like.

MATERIALS: Unger Fluffy baby yarn (1.75 oz./50 gram balls)—1 each of color A (green), B (blue), C (white); 2 balls of D (pink).

Knitting Needles: #9 (5.5 mm) or size needed for correct gauge.

GAUGE: 9 sts = 2 inch.

DIRECTIONS

Using A, cast on 119 stitches. Work 9 rows of seed stitch (*k 1, p 1, repeat from * across row).

Row 10: With A (k 1, p 1) 3 times. Change to B (back side) and p to last 6 sts. Change back to A and (p 1, k 1) 3 times.

Row 11: Continuing with A, (k 1, p 1) 3 times, then change to B and k across row, changing to A for the last 6 stitches. K 1, p 1 to end.

Rows 12, 14, 16, & 18: With A (k 1, p 1) 3 times. Change to C and p to last 6 sts. Change back to A, (p 1, k 1) 3 times.

Rows 13, 15, & 17: With A, (k 1, p 1) 3 times. Change to C and k across row. Change to A for the last 6 sts. K 1, p 1 to end.

Row 19: With A, (k 1, p 1) 3 times, change to B, k 6. Change to C, k 95 sts, change to B, k 6, change to A, (p 1, k 1) 3 times.

Row 20: With A, (k 1, p 1) 3 times. Change to B, p 6, change to C, p 95. Change to B, p 6, change to A, (p 1, k 1) 3 times.

Rows 21, 23, 25 & 27: Work same as Row 19.

Rows 22, 24, & 26: Work same as Row 20.

Row 28: Using A, (k 1, p 1) 3 times. Change to B, p 6, change to C, p 6. Change to D, p 83. Change to C, p 6, change to B, p 6, change to A, (p 1, k 1) 3 times.
Begin leaf pattern over the D stitches, keeping A, B, and C stitches the same.

Leaf Pattern

ABBREVIATIONS:

ssk = slip, slip, knit. Slip the next 2 stitches one at a time onto the right-hand needle without working them. Then insert the tip of the left-hand needle into the fronts of these 2 stitches and knit 2 together. s2sk = same as ssk, except that the first 2 stitches are slipped tog and the third is slipped by itself. The tip of the left-hand needle is then inserted into the front of all 3 stitches, which are then knit tog.

Row 1: K 1, ssk, * k 3, yo, k 1, yo, k 3, slip 2, slip 1 and knit all 3. Rep from * and end k 2 tog, k 1.

Row 2 and all even rows through row 16: Purl all stitches.

Row 3: K 1, ssk, * k 2, yo, k 3, yo, k 2, s2sk, rep from *.

Row 5: K 1, ssk, * k 1, yo, k 5, yo, k 1, s2sk, rep from * and end with k 2 tog, k 1.

Row 7: K 1, ssk, * yo, k 7, yo, s2sk, and end with yo, k 1.

Row 9: K 2, *yo, k 3, s2sk, k 3, yo, k 1, rep from * and end with yo, k 2.

Row 11: K 3, *yo, k 2, s2sk, k 2, yo, k 3, rep from * and end with yo, k 3.

Row 13: K 4, * yo, k 1, s2sk, k 1, yo, k 5, rep from * and end with yo, k 4.

Row 15: K 5, * yo, s2sk, yo, k 7, rep from * and end with yo, k 5.
Repeat these 16 rows until you have completed 9 leaves.

TO FINISH
Begin with Row 27 and work back to Row 1 to finish the afghan in the same way as you started.

VARIATION NO. 1

A – blue
B – yellow
C – white
D – aqua

VARIATION NO. 2

A – medium green
B – light green
C – white
D – yellow

WHITE ARAN

*T*here is nothing quite so pretty as a white afghan with an interesting stitch to give it texture. This one is 54 × 61 inches, which is perfect for a single bed. Made with Unger's Utopia, it takes only 14 skeins of yarn.

This one would look equally good in a dark forest green or an earthy, autumn rust. There are so many beautiful shades of pastels as well. Consider the various blues or lavenders. Choosing a color that's just right for you is half the fun of creating a project, and there is quite a range to pick from.

MATERIALS: Unger's Utopia 4-ply acrylic (3.5 oz./100 gram skeins)—14 skeins white.

Crochet Hook: #10/J (6 mm) or size needed for correct gauge.

GAUGE: 7 sc = 2 inches; 7 rows = 2 inches. Each motif measures 10½ × 11½ inches.

DIRECTIONS

Puff (P) Stitch: Yo, insert hook from front to back to front around post or bar which is in the upright position of st, pull up a lp to height of row, yo, insert hook around post of same st, pull up a lp, yo and through 4 lps, yo and through 2 lps.

Dropped Bobble (DB): With last lp of each st held on hook, insert hook behind the piece (to right side of work) and into the free lp of st 2 rows below, work 3 dc in lp, yo and through 4 lps on hook.

Joined Puff (JP) Stitch: Work puff st around post of same sc 2 rows below working to the last lp of st (2 lps rem on hook), sk next sc 2 rows below, puff st to last lp around post of next sc behind st just made.

Motif (Make 25.)

NOTE: Work each sc in *back lp only* throughout.
Ch 26.

Row 1 (right side): Sc in 2nd ch from hook and in each ch (25 ch). Ch 1, turn.

Row 2: Sc in each st. Ch 1, turn.

Row 3: Sc in first 2 sc, * P st in next st 2 rows below, sk sc behind P st, sc in next sc, P st in next st, sk sc behind P st *, sc in next 15 sc. Rep from * to * once, sc in last 2 sc. Ch 1, turn.

Row 4: Sc in first 12 sts, DB in front lp of next st 2 rows below, sk sc in front of DB, sc in last 12 sts. Ch 1, turn.

Row 5: Sc in 2 sc, * P st in P st, sk sc behind P st, sc in next sc, P st in next P st, sk sc behind P st *, sc in next 15 sts. Rep from * to * once, sc in last 2 sc. Ch 1, turn.

Row 6: Sc in first 10 sts, (DB in next st, sk sc in front, sc in next st), turn.

Rows 7, 9, 11, & 13: Rep Row 5.

Row 8: Sc in each st. Ch 1, turn.

Row 10: Rep Row 4.

Row 12: Sc in first 10 sts, DB in next st, sk sc in front, sc in 3 sc, DB in next st, sk sc in front, sc in last 10 sc. Ch 1, turn.

Row 14: Sc in 8 sc, (DB in next st, sk sc in front, sc in 3 sc) twice, DB in next st, sk sc in front, sc in last 8 sc. Ch 1, turn.

Row 15: Sc in first 2 sc. Rep from * to * of Row 5 once, sc in next 2 sc, P st in next st 2 rows below, sk sc behind P st, sc in next 9 sts, P st in next st 2 rows below, sk sc behind P st, sc in next 2 sts. Rep from * to * of Row 5 once, sc in last 2 sc. Ch 1, turn.

Row 16: Rep Row 14.

Row 17 and all other odd-numbered rows: Rep Row 5.

Row 18: Rep Row 12.

Row 20: Rep Row 4.

Row 22: Rep Row 8.

Row 24: Rep Row 6.

Row 26: Rep Row 4.

Row 28: Rep Row 8. Ch 1, turn.

Border

Rnd 1: Work 3 sc in first sc (corner), work 21 sc across to last st, 3 sc in last st (corner), 23 sc across next edge to next corner, 3 sc in corner, 21 sc across next edge to next corner, 23 sc across last edge, join to first sc (100 sc). Ch 1, turn.

Rnds 2 & 3: Sc in back lp of each st around and work 3 sc in each corner st. At end of last row join, do not turn.

Rnd 4: Ch 1, sc in both lps of each st around, with 3 sc in each corner st, join (124 sc).

Rnd 5: Ch 1, sc in joining, JP st over next 3 sts 2 rows below, sk 2 sc behind JP st, * sc in next sc, 3 sc in corner st, sc in next sc, (JP st, sc in next 3 sc) 5 times, JP st, sc in next sc, 3 sc in corner st, sc in next sc, (JP st, sc in next 3 sc) twice, JP st, sc in next 5 sc, JP st, (sc in next 3 sc, JP st) twice. Rep from * around. Join. Ch 1, turn.

Rnd 6: Sc in back lp of each st, with 3 sc in each corner st. Join. Fasten off.

TO FINISH
Sew 5 × 5-inch motifs together.

Edging: From right side, join yarn in a corner, sc evenly around entire outer edge with 3 sc in each corner st, join. Fasten off.

Bobble Repeat

*T*he combination of the textured stitch and the varying shades of blue make this an interesting project. You can use different shades of one color in any color desired to match your room or preference. The sketch shows a combination of warm autumn colors. When choosing yarns, be sure to buy all of the same weight and manufacturer. The finished afghan is 51 × 70 inches, not including fringe.

MATERIALS: Bernat Berella "4" knitting worsted (3.5 oz./100 gram balls)—3 each of color A (colonial blue) and color D (pale colonial blue); 5 each of color B (medium colonial blue) and color C (light colonial blue).

Crochet Hook: #10½/K (6.5 mm) or size needed for correct gauge.

GAUGE: 5 sts = 2 inches; 3 rows = 1 inch.

DIRECTIONS

NOTE: The abbreviation used in the following directions is preceded by the explanation the first time it appears. For example, in Row 2 of pattern st, the directions for bobble directly precede this abbreviation. They are: yo hook, draw up a loop in next st, (yo, draw up a loop in same st) twice, yo, pull through all 7 loops on hook.

Pattern Stitch

Row 1: Using color A, 1 sc in 2nd ch from hook, 1 sc in each remaining ch st—175 sts.

Row 2: Using color A, ch 1, turn, 1 sc in each of next 3 sts; * yo hook, draw up a lp in next st, (yo, draw up a lp in same st) twice, yo, pull through all 7 lps on hook (bobble); 1 sc in each of next 3 sts, repeat from * across row.

Rows 3 & 5: Using color A, ch 1, turn, 1 sc in each st across row.

Row 4: Using color A, ch 1, turn, 1 sc in first st, bobble in next st, * 1 sc in each of next 3 sts, bobble in next st, repeat from *, ending 1 sc in last st.

Row 6: Repeat Row 2, break off color A; draw color B through last 2 lps of last sc worked.

Rows 7 through 11: Using color B, repeat Rows 3 through 5, then repeat Rows 2 and 3.

Row 12: Using color B, repeat Row 4, break off color B; draw color C through last 2 lps of last sc worked.

Rows 13 through 17: Using color C, repeat Row 3, then repeat Rows 2 through 5.

Row 18: Using color C, repeat Row 2, break off color C; draw color D through last 2 lps of last sc worked.

Rows 19 through 23: Using color D, repeat Rows 3 through 5, then repeat Rows 2 and 3.

Row 24: Using color D, repeat Row 4, break off color D; draw color C through last 2 lps of last sc worked.

Rows 25 through 29: Using color C, repeat Row 3, then repeat Rows 2 through 5.

Row 30: Using color C, repeat Row 2, break off color C; draw color B through last 2 lps of last sc worked.

Rows 31 through 35: Using color B, repeat Rows 3 through 5, then repeat Rows 2 and 3.

Row 36: Using color B, repeat Row 4, break off color B; draw color A through last 2 lps of last sc worked.

Row 37: Repeat Row 3.
Repeat Rows 2 through 37 for pattern stitch.
Using color A, ch 176 sts. Work even until pattern st has been worked 4 times, ending with Row 37 of pattern st. Then work Rows 2 through 5, then repeat Rows 2 and 3 once more. Fasten off.

TO FINISH

Fringe: Cut strands of yarn 7 inches long. Matching colors, knot 4 strands in every bobble row across each side. Trim ends.

VARIATION NO. 1

A – wine
B – cherry red
C – pink
D – peach

VARIATION NO. 2

A – dark brown
B – burnt sienna
C – deep orange
D – yellow

Spring Garden

*S*ince this pretty afghan is made in panels, it's easy to manage. When all panels are finished, you simply stitch them together to create the garden motif. The design is worked in cross-stitch by following the graph for each section.

The yarn is completely washable. Make this afghan for use on a cool summer night or as a lap throw in the wintertime. What could be more refreshing than flowers in winter?

This, like the Victorian Rose afghan on page 150, makes a very special wedding gift to treasure. The finished project is 53 × 64 inches.

MATERIALS: Unger's Utopia 4-ply acrylic (3.5 oz./100 gram balls)— 9 balls of MC (white); 2 balls each of color A (plum) and B (lavender); 1 ball each of C (dark blue), D (dark green), E (light green), F (light blue).

Crochet Hook: #10/J (6 mm) or size needed for correct gauge.
Yarn needle.

GAUGE: 7 sts = 2 inches; 3 rows = 1 inch.

DIRECTIONS

Center Panel (28 × 38 inches)
With MC, ch 98.

Row 1 First Half: Pull up a lp onto hook in each ch across (98 lps).

Second Half: Yo and pull through 1 lp, * yo and pull through 2 lps; rep from * across (1 lp).

Row 2 First Half: Pull up a lp in each st, inserting hook under vertical bar (98 lps).

Second Half: Same as second half of Row 1 (1 lp made). Repeat Row 2 for afghan st pat until piece measures 38 inches. End on second half of row.

Finishing Row: *Pull up a lp under vertical bar and through lp on hook. Rep from * across. Fasten off.

Side Panels (Make 2, 10 × 38 inches.)
With MC, ch 35. Work in afghan st pat until piece measures 38 inches. Fasten off.

End Panels (Make 2, 10 × 48 inches.)
With MC, ch 35. Work in afghan st pat until piece measures 48 inches. Fasten off.

TO FINISH

Mark center of center panel for center motif.

Embroidery: Work in cross-stitch throughout. Follow Chart 1 for the center-panel motif.

Follow Chart 2 for the side edges of the center panel. Work 2 motifs on each long side, 5 stitches in from edge. Alternate main flower colors.

Follow Chart 3 for the side panels. Work 2 motifs on each panel, 8 sts in from edge. Alternate main flower color with corresponding flowers of center panel.

Follow Chart 3 for end panels. Center 1 motif on each panel, 8 sts in from edge.

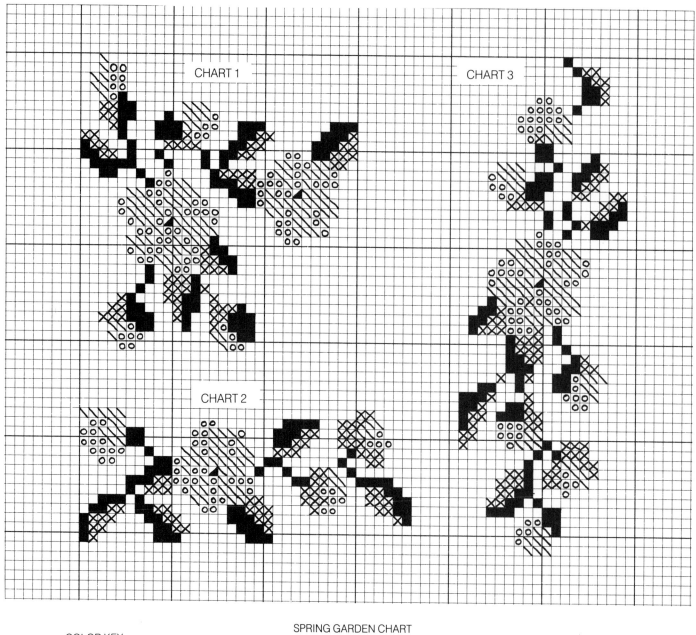

SPRING GARDEN CHART

COLOR KEY

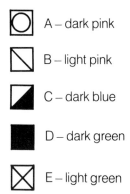

A – dark pink

B – light pink

C – dark blue

D – dark green

E – light green

Alternate Flower

F – (light blue)
G – (dark blue)

64

Edging

Row 1: From wrong side, join A in corner of center panel to work across long edge, sc in same place, * ch 1, sk ⅜" along edge, sc in edge. Rep from * across, end with sc in next corner. Ch 1, turn.

Row 2 (right side): Working in *front lps only,* * in next sc, work sc, ch 1, dc, ch 1, and sc, sl st in next sc (shell made). Rep from * across, end with sl st in last sc. Fasten off. Rep edging on rem long edge.

Sewing: Sew side panels to long edges of center front panel using rem free lps of Row 1 of edging. Work edging across narrow ends of afghan, beg at corner of a side panel and across center and rem side panel. Fasten off. Sew end panels to free lps of edgings just worked.

Border

Rnd 1: From wrong side, join A in a corner. Work same as for Row 1 of edging all around entire outer edge, working sc and ch. Rep 70 times across top and bottom edges, 88 times across each side edge with a sc in each corner. End with ch 1, join to first sc. Ch 1 and turn.

Rnd 2: Work same as for Row 2 of edging with a shell at each corner. Join. Change to B.

Rnd 3: * Ch 2, sc in dc of next shell, ch 2, sl st in next sl st bet shells. Rep from * around, end with ch 2, join to first ch.

Rnd 4: Sl st into first ch sp, ch 3, dc in same sp, in next ch sp of next shell, in next sc work dc, ch 1, tr, ch 1, and dc, 2 dc in next ch sp of same shell, (sc in next ch sp) twice. Rep from * around. Join to top of beg ch.

Rnd 5: Ch 2, * work 2 hdc in first dc at point of shell, hdc in next ch sp, 4 hdc in center tr, hdc in next ch sp, sk next dc, 2 hdc in next dc, ch 1, sk next dc and sc, sc in next sc, ch 1. Skip next 2 dc. Rep from * around. Join. Fasten off.

VARIATION NO. 1

A – dark rose
B and F – light rose
C and D – dark green
E – light green

VARIATION NO. 2

A – yellow ochre
B and F – yellow
C and D – dark green
E – light green

Winter Granny

I gave this afghan its name because it has a wintery look. The blue and brown colors give it a warm and cozy feeling and the cherry red brightens up the color scheme. It is one of my favorite combinations.

The yarn is an acrylic/wool blend and is so soft to the touch that you'd never know it was part synthetic. My mother, Ruth Linsley, did the crochet work and said this project was especially easy and portable since each square is made separately and then stitched together when all are finished. The squares are an ample 8 inches and the finished afghan is 50 × 66 inches, including the 1-inch border all around.

MATERIALS: Phildar Prognostic (1.75 oz./50 gram skeins)—6 skeins each of A (red), B (light blue), C (dark blue), D (camel).

Crochet Hook: #8/H (5 mm) or size needed for correct gauge.

GAUGE: Each motif = 8 × 8 inches.

DIRECTIONS

Make 12 squares of each color. Begin with ch 6. Join with sl st to form ring.

Rnd 1: Ch 3, (yo, insert hook in ring and draw up lp, yo and draw through 2 lps on hook) 2 times, yo and draw through all 3 lps on hook (first cl made), * ch 5 (yo, insert hook in ring and draw up lp, yo and draw through 2 lps on hook) 3 times, yo and draw through all 4 lps on hook (another cl made), ch 1, work cl. Rep from * 2 times more, ch 5, work cl, ch 1, join with sl st in top of first cl.

Rnd 2: Sl st in next ch-5 sp, work first cl in same sp, ch 3, work another cl in same space (first corner made), * ch 1, work 3 dc in next ch-1 sp, ch 1, in next ch-5 sp work cl, ch 3, and cl (another corner made). Rep from * 2 times more, ch 1, work 3 dc in next sp, ch 1, join to first cl.

Rnd 3: Sl st in next ch-3 sp, work first corner in same sp, * ch 2, dc in next sp, dc in each of next 3 dc, dc in next sp, ch 2, work corner in next sp. Rep from * 2 times more. Ch 2, dc in next sp, dc in each of next 3 dc, dc in next sp, ch 2, join.

Rnd 4: Sl st in next ch-3 sp, work first corner in same sp, * ch 2, dc in next sp and in each dc to next sp, dc in sp, ch 2, work corner in next sp. Rep from * 2 times more, ch 2, dc in next sp, dc in each dc to next sp, dc in sp, ch 2, join.

Rnd 5: Rep Rnd 4.

TO FINISH
Arrange rows of 6 across and 8 down as follows:

```
A  B  C  D  A  B
D  A  B  C  D  A
C  D  A  B  C  D
B  C  D  A  B  C
A  B  C  D  A  B
D  A  B  C  D  A
C  D  A  B  C  D
B  C  D  A  B  C
```

Join tog from the wrong side with a sc through each pair of corresponding dc, picking up *back lps only* of dc and working 1 sc in corner sps.

After all squares are joined, attach yarn to a square after a 3-dc cl in the ch-2 sp.

Rnd 1: Ch 3 (first dc), 1 dc in each dc of square. Work 1 dc in ch-2 sp, ch 2, 1 cl as in squares in corner, ch 2, 1 cl in corner, ch 2.

Continue in this way all around the afghan. Join with a sl st in ch 3 (first dc). When you come to each of 4 corners, work 2 cls separated by a ch 3.

69

Rnd 2: Ch 3 (first dc), work 1 dc in each of the next 10 dc, *1 dc in ch-2 sp, ch 2 (1 cl of 5 joined), dc in ch-2 sp, ch 2, 1 dc in ch-2 sp, 11 dc.* Rep around between *s, ending with sl st into the 3rd ch of the first dc. Fasten off.

VARIATION NO. 1

A – light blue
B – light pink
C – light green
D – light yellow

VARIATION NO. 2

A – dark red
B – purple
C – dark green
D – dark blue

Quilt Squares

*B*ased on a patchwork-designed quilt, this crochet pattern is created by joining triangles of light and dark colors to create light and dark squares. I chose various shades of red with white because these colors were traditionally used for early quilts. As you can see from the sketches, alternate colors can be just as pretty. The finished throw is approximately 47 inches square.

MATERIALS: Phildar Pegase knitting worsted (1.75 oz./50 gram balls)—2 balls of color A (dark red); 5 balls each of colors B (bright red) and D (pink); 6 balls each of colors C (wine) and E (white).

Crochet Hook: #8/H (5 mm) or size needed for correct gauge. Tapestry needle.

GAUGE: Each square = 4½ inches.

DIRECTIONS

NOTE: Each square is made up of a 2-color combination. The directions are the same for each square; the color combinations vary. The following are the number of squares needed for each color variation.

Colors A/C—16 squares
Colors B/D—16 squares
Colors B/E—4 squares
Colors B/C—20 squares
Colors C/E—16 squares
Colors D/E—28 squares

Beginning with any color, ch 2.

Row 1: 3 sc in 2nd ch from hook, ch 1, turn.

Row 2: 2 sc in first sc (inc made), sc in each sc, 2 sc in last sc (inc made), ch 1, turn.

Row 3: Work 2 sc in first sc, sc in each sc, work 2 sc in last sc, ch 1, turn.
Repeat Row 3 nine times (25 sts).

Row 13: Join second color in last lp of last sc, ch 1, turn. Sc in each sc (25 sts of second color).

Row 14: Decrease 1 sc at both ends of each row until 1 sc remains. End off.

TO FINISH

Follow chart to assemble. Sew squares together.

Edging: Using color C, sc all around. Change to color B. Starting at a corner, shell stitch (in first sc, dc 4 times). Sc in next 3 sc. In next sc, shell stitch. Continue all the way around for scalloped edge.

Blocking: If possible, place the throw on a carpet and pin each corner. Go over it very lightly with a steam iron to block. Leave until throw is "set," about a half-hour. If you don't have a carpeted area, pad a tabletop with towels and place the throw on top. Steam press to block.

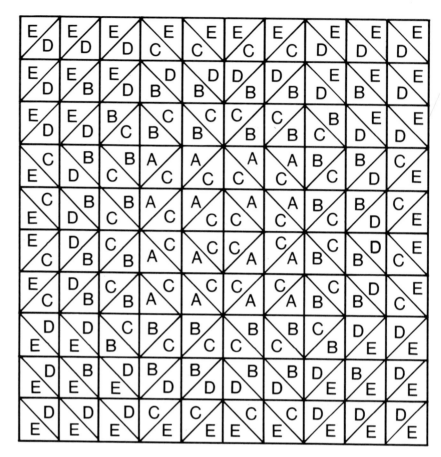

QUILT SQUARES CHART

VARIATION NO. 1

A – orange
B – red
C – copper
D – white
E – yellow

VARIATION NO. 2

A – navy blue
B – dark blue
C – sky blue
D – light blue
E – white

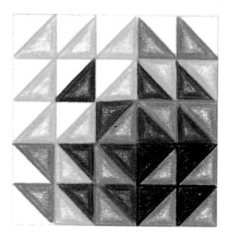

Daisy Crib Cover

*T*he finished size of this little afghan is 27 × 34, which is just right for a carriage or crib cover. If you'd like to enlarge it, simply add more daisy rounds. This bright and cheerful afghan of yellow-and-white daisies on a field of green was designed by Tillie Sparrow for Crystal Palace Yarns. It is made of 50/50 cotton/acrylic and is completely washable. Change the daisies to black-eyed Susans by following the color changes in the sketch.

MATERIALS: Crystal Palace Sunshine (1.75 oz./50 gram balls/101 yards)—1 ball A (yellow), 5 balls B (white), 7 balls C (green).

Crochet Hook: #6/G (4.5 mm) or size needed for correct gauge.

GAUGE: One motif measures approximately 2½ inches square.

DIRECTIONS

Check your gauge before beginning and adjust your hook size to obtain motif size shown. If you want to make the daisy cover a little larger, use a #8/H hook.

Make 154 daisy motifs.

Using A, ch 4 and join into a ring with a slip st in the first ch.

Rnd 1: Ch 1, 8 sc into ring, join with sl st to first ch. Break off A.

Rnd 2: Join in B to any sc, sl st into same place as join, (4 ch, leaving last lp of each tr on hook, work 2 tr into same place as last sl st, yo and draw through all 3 lps, 4 ch, sl st into same place as last sl st—petal worked—sl st into next sc) 8 times, working sl st at end of last repeat in same sc as join. Break off B.

Rnd 3: Join in C to top of any petal, (1 sc into top of petal, 3 ch, 1 sc into top of next petal, 5 ch) 4 times, join with a sl st to first sc.

Rnd 4: 1 sc into same place as sl st, (1 sc into each of next 3 ch, 1 sc into next sc, 1 sc into each of next 2 ch, 1 sc into next 2 ch) 4 times, omitting 1 sc at end of last repeat. Join with a sl st to form first sc. Fasten off.

TO FINISH

Sew the daisy motifs together with 11 across and 14 down. Work 1 row sc, then a row of dc, then a row of sc around the edge. Steam lightly on the back, but do not press or you will flatten the daisies. This afghan can be washed in a machine and dried on delicate cycle. If hand-washing is preferred, dry flat.

VARIATION NO. 1

A – orange
B – white
C – brown

VARIATION NO. 2

A – brown
B – yellow
C – blue

Candlewick Crochet

*E*veryone appreciates a natural-color afghan because it goes with everything in any room. But this pattern would look just as pretty in a pastel, which would show off the stitches. It makes a wonderfully special wedding gift.

The finished size is approximately 48 × 72 inches, not including the fringe.

MATERIALS: Bernat Berella "4" knitting worsted (3.5 oz./100 gram balls)—14 Natural.

Crochet Hook: #10½/K (7 mm) or size needed for correct gauge.

GAUGE: 3 sc = 1 inch; 3 rows = 1 inch.

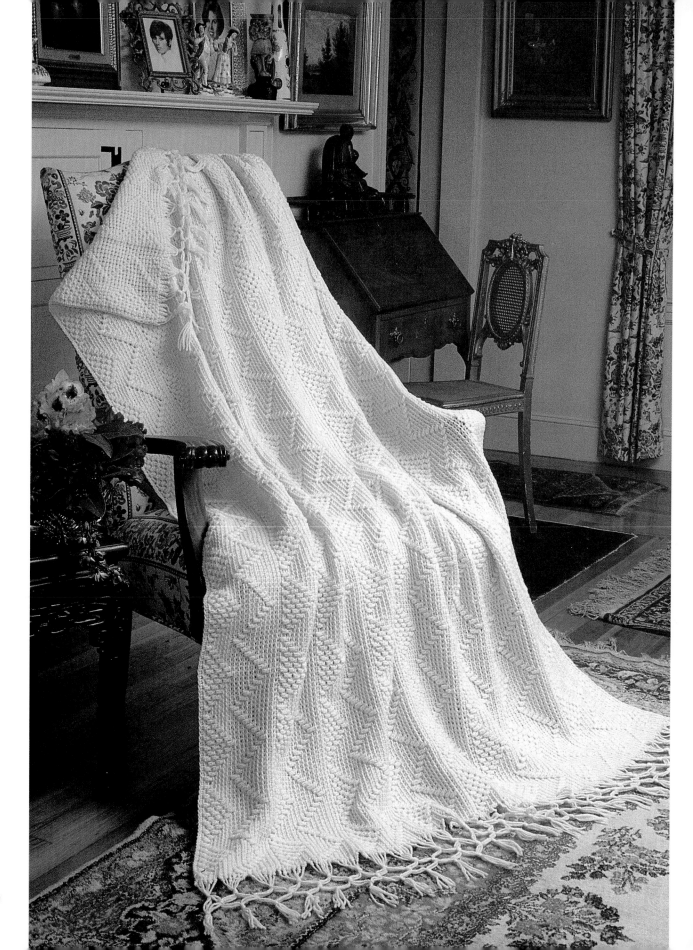

DIRECTIONS

NOTE 1: *Every row* is worked with right side facing you.

NOTE 2: At beg of *every row*, leave a 10-inch end for fringe, then ch 3 before working sts on the chart. At the end of *every row* after working sts on chart, ch 3, then fasten off, leaving a 10-inch end for fringe.

NOTE 3: Except for Row 2 of afghan, work sc in *back loop only*.

NOTE 4: Explanation of abbreviation used on chart: Long front st—with yarn held in *front* of work, yo hook, insert hook under remaining loop of next st 2 rows below, and draw up a loop, (yo and pull through 2 loops) twice.

Row 1: Leaving a 10-inch end, ch 217 sts; fasten off, leaving a 10-inch end.

Row 2: Leaving a 10-inch end, ch 3; working in ch sts of Row 1, 1 sc in 4th st of ch, 1 sc in each st of ch to last 3 sts, ch 3; fasten off, leaving a 10-inch end—211 sc plus ch 3 at beg and end of row.

Row 3: Leaving a 10-inch end, ch 3, working in *back loop only*, 1 sc in each sc, ch 3, fasten off, leaving a 10-inch end.

Now work as follows: Leaving a 10-inch end, ch 3, work Row 1 of chart on 211 sts, ch 3, and fasten off, leaving a 10-inch end. Continue to follow chart for design on 211 sts until the chart has been worked 8 times, ending with Row 17, then repeat Rows 1 through 7 once more, and repeat Row 17 once.

TO FINISH

Row 1: Separate 10-inch ends into groups of 6 strands, except at beg and end of afghan, where you separate into groups of 7 strands. Knot each group of strands tog approximately 1½ inches from the last ch st.

Rows 2 & 3: Separate 3 strands from each of 2 adjoining knots and knot these strands tog approximately 1½ inches from previous knots. Trim ends.

CANDLEWICK CHART

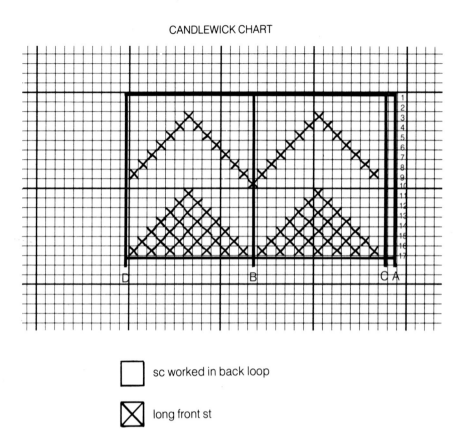

□   sc worked in back loop

☒   long front st

All rows are right-side rows and are worked (and read on the chart) from right to left. Start at A, work to B, repeat between C and B, end between B and D.

MoHair Stripe

*T*he yarn used for this afghan, designed by Amelie Oldham, is a blend of mohair, wool, silk, and nylon from Tahki. It is soft and lightweight with lots of warmth. While the skeins are only 50 grams each, this yarn goes a long way, especially when worked with #10 needles. There are approximately 187 yards to a skein, which is considerably more than you'll get from a 100-gram skein of a heavier yarn. The finished size is 63 × 84 inches.

MATERIALS: Tahki Ltd. Saratoga (1.75 oz./50 gram skeins)—10 skeins MC (green), 1 skein each of colors A (yellow), B (royal blue), C (red), D (navy blue), E (mauve).

Knitting Needles: #10 (6 mm) or size needed for correct gauge.

GAUGE: 4 sts = 1 inch; 6 rows = 1 inch.

DIRECTIONS

Using main color (MC) cast on 164 sts.

Rows 1 through 26: K 2, p 2 across each row. Change to A.

Rows 27 through 30: K across. Change to MC.

Rows 31 & 32: K 2, p 2 across. Change to B.

Rows 33 through 36: K across each row. Change to MC.

Rows 37 through 40: K 2, p 2 across each row. Change to C.

Rows 41 through 44: K across. Change to MC.

Rows 45 through 48: K 2, p 2 across. Change to D.

Rows 49 through 52: K across. Change to MC.

Rows 53 & 54: K 2, p 2 across. Change to E.

Rows 55 through 58: K across. Change to MC.

Rows 59 through 62: K 2, p 2 across. Change to A.

Rows 63 through 66: K across. Change to MC.

Next 24 rows: K 2, p 2 across. Change back to A.

Next 2 rows: K across. Change to E.

Next 2 rows: K across. Change to D.

Next 2 rows: K across. Change to C.

Next 2 rows: K across. Change to B.

Next 2 rows: K across. Change to A.

Next 4 rows: K across. Change to MC.

Next 4 rows: With MC k 2, p 2 across each row. Change to color E.

Next 4 rows: K across. Change to MC.

Next 2 rows: K across. Change to D.

Next 4 rows: K across. Change to MC.

Next 4 rows: K 2, p 2 across. Change to C.

Next 4 rows: K across. Change to MC.

Next 4 rows: K 2, p 2 across. Change to B.

Next 4 rows: K across. Change to MC.

Next 4 rows: K 2, p 2 across. Change to A.

Next 4 rows: K across. Change to MC.

Next 26 rows: K 2, p 2 across.

VARIATION NO. 1

MC – lavender
A – light blue
B and D – burgundy
C – fuchsia
E – royal blue

VARIATION NO. 2

MC – pale blue
A – ochre
B and D – navy blue
C – red
E – royal blue

Baby Plaid

*C*uddle *your baby in this soft knit afghan, which looks and feels like mohair but is completely washable and will look like new every time. At 34 × 42 inches, it is ample for a crib or to use in a carriage. This one is made with Unger's Fluffy in white, pink, and blue, but this yarn comes in a wide variety of colors so you can choose the color combination that suits you best.*

MATERIALS: Unger's Fluffy baby yarn (50 gram balls/1.75 oz. balls)— 5 balls A (white), 1 each B (pink) and C (blue).

Needles: #17 or size needed for correct gauge.

Crochet Hook: K

GAUGE: 4 pat sts using double strand = 2 inches; 5 rows = 2 inches. NOTE: Work with 2 strands held tog throughout. Horizontal lines are worked in and vertical lines are crocheted on later.

DIRECTIONS

With A, cast on 85 sts. Knit 3 rows for garter stitch border. Change to seed stitch.

Seed Stitch Pattern:

Row 1: K 1, * p 1, k 1; Rep from * across. Rep this row for pat. You will always work a k over a p and a p over a k.

Next, * work 8 rows A, 2 rows B, 8 rows A, 2 rows C. Rep from * until 4th C stripe has been completed (80 pat rows in all). Work even until the 10th A stripe is completed. K 3 rows. Bind off as to knit.

Cross Lines: Beg at lower edge of afghan above garter st border. Join a double strand of B in 7th st from side edge. With yarn coming from wrong side, and crochet hook on right side, sl st in each row to beg of garter st border. Fasten off B.

Skip 8 sts at lower edge, join a double strand of C in next st above garter st border and work a row of sl st as for first stripe. Alternate colors B and C and continue to work a stripe, as established, in every 9th st until the 5th B stripe has been completed.

Right Half: * skip next 8 sts. Make next st a cross stripe, sk next 8 sts, make next st a B cross stripe; rep from * once.

Work **Left Half** in same way.

VARIATION NO. 1
A – light yellow
B – green
C – peach

VARIATION NO. 2
A – baby blue
B – blue
C – red

Easy Lap Throw

*T*his afghan can be completed in less than a weekend. You are creating just one ever-increasing square to make one large granny. The interest comes from the change of colors to create borders for this 60-inch square. For an alternate color scheme, use shades of blue and follow the directions as given.

MATERIALS: Sport-weight yarn (3.5 oz./100 gram balls)—5 skeins of A (red), 3 skeins of B (yellow), 4 skeins of C (blue).

Crochet Hook: #10/J (6 mm) or size needed for correct gauge.

GAUGE: 16 sts (4 groups of 3 dc, ch 1) = 6 inches.

DIRECTIONS

Rnd 1: Beg at center with A, ch 3, work 2 dc in 3rd ch from hook (counts as 3 dc), ch 2, * 3 dc in same ch, ch 2, rep from * twice. Join with a sl st in top of starting ch (4 grps of 3 dc).

Rnd 2: Ch 3, 2 dc in joining sl st (half corner), ch 1, * 3 dc, ch 2, 3 dc in next sp (corner), ch 1, rep from * twice, half corner of 3 dc in last sp, ch 2, sl st in top of starting ch 3 (8 groups of 3 dc) (4 corners).

Rnd 3: Ch 3, 2 dc in joining sl st, ch 1 (half corner); * 3 dc in next ch-1 sp, ch 1, corner of 3 dc, ch 2, 3 dc in next corner sp, ch 1. Repeat from * twice, 3 dc in next ch-1 sp, ch 1, half corner of 3 dc in last sp, ch 2, sl st in top of starting ch 3.

Rnd 4: Ch 3, work half corner of 3 dc in corner sp, ch 1, * 3 dc in next ch-1 sp, ch 1, repeat from * to corner sp, work corner of 3 dc, ch 2, 3 dc in corner sp, ch 1. Repeat from first * twice, work 3 dc, ch 1 in each ch-1 sp to next corner sp, work half corner of 3 dc, ch 2, join with sl st in top of first st.

Rnd 5: Ch 3, 2 dc in joining sl st (half corner), ch 1, work from first * on Rnd 4.

Rnd 6: Repeat Rnd 4.

Rnd 7: Repeat Rnd 4 and fasten off.

Rnd 8: With B, rep Rnd 5 eight times.

Rnd 16: With C, rep Rnd 5 eight times.

Rnd 24: With A, rep Rnds 4 and 5 eight times.

Rnd 40: With B, rep Rnds 4 and 5 eight times.

Rnd 56: With C, rep Rnds 4 and 5 eight times.

Rnd 72: With A, rep Rnds 4 and 5 twice. Fasten off.

TO FINISH

Run in all yarn ends on the wrong side. With A, work one row of sc around outside edge.

VARIATION NO. 1

A – red
B – bright blue
C – white

VARIATION NO. 2

A – dark blue
B – medium blue
C – light blue

Pastel Cotton

*T*his afghan is made in 5 strips. Each strip measures 8 × 48 inches and the finished size is 40 × 48 inches. Bee Gonnella designed this project using lightweight, soft cotton yarn in light, airy colors. The sketches show how different it would look in different colors.

MATERIALS: Conshohocken cotton (3.5 oz./100 gram balls)—2 balls each color: A (lavender), B (white), C (green), D (yellow), E (rose), F (peach).

Knitting Needles: #9 (5.5 mm) or size needed for correct gauge.

Crochet hook.
2 large bobbins.

GAUGE: 4 stockinette sts = 1 inch; 6 rows = 1 inch.

VARIATION NO. 1

A, D, F – royal blue
C and E – light blue
B – white

DIRECTIONS

Panel 1

Cast on 32 sts in A as MC. Work 35 rows in stockinette st (knit 1 row, purl 1 row).

Row 36: Add B (white) yarn and follow Chart B through Row 48.

Row 49: Change MC to C and work the next 48 rows following Charts D and B.

Row 97: Change MC to D and follow Charts D and B for 48 rows. The following 48 rows are worked in colors E and F. The last 48 rows are worked with A.

Panel 2

Cast on 32 sts in color F. Work 35 rows. Follow Charts A and B.

Row 49: Change MC to A and follow Charts C, D, A, and B.

Next 48 rows: Work the MC in C, followed by D, E, and F.

Last 48 rows: Follow Charts C and D, ending with 35 rows worked in color F.

Panel 3

Work same as for Panel 2, but begin and end with color E, then follow the colors in order.

Panel 4

Begin and end with D.

Panel 5

Begin with color C and work 35 rows. Work the next 13 rows following Chart A. Change to color D and follow Charts C and A. End with color C and follow Chart C working the last 35 rows in color C.

TO FINISH

Working left to right, sew panels 1, 2, 3, 4, and 5 tog. With B (white), work 2 rows of single crochet around the edge of the entire afghan.

VARIATION NO. 2

A – tan
B – white
C – dark red
D – brown
E – olive green
F – burnt umber

PASTEL COTTON CHART

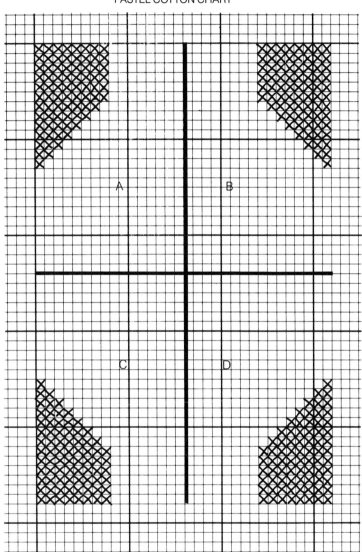

Start A, work to B, repeat between C and B once, end between C and D.

COUNTRY HEARTS

*M*ade up of gray and white with red hearts, this delightful and simple-to-knit afghan measures approximately 63 × 66 inches and is perfect for a single bed. It's made with an acrylic yarn that is as soft as any wool, yet is washable. I like this yarn for large projects such as afghans.

MATERIALS: Phildar Quality Leader knitting worsted (3.5 oz./100 gram balls)—11 balls of color A (gray), 6 balls of color B (white), 1 ball of color C (red).

Knitting Needles: #8 (5 mm) or size needed for correct gauge.

GAUGE: Stockinette st: 19 sts = 4 inches; 27 rows = 4 inches.

Stockinette Stitch (St st): K 1 row, p 1 row. Following the chart, repeat 2 rows for the Fair Isle pattern.
Embroider with duplicate stitch (see page 20).

DIRECTIONS

Motif A (Make 7 using color A, and 4 using color B.)
With background color, cast on 39 sts. Work in St st for 54 rows. Bind off. Follow Chart A and embroider the heart with color C.

Motif B (Make 6 with color B as background color and color A as contrast color; make 4 with color A as background color and color B as contrast color.)
With color B cast on 39 sts. Work 8 rows in St st. Following Chart B:

Row 9: With B color K 7, with A color K 2, * with B k 2, with A k 2; rep from * 5 times more; with B k 6.

Row 10: With B p 6, with A p 2, * with B p 2, with A p 2; rep from * 5 times more; with B p 7.

Row 11: With B k 9, * with A k 2, with B k 2; rep from * 4 times more; with A k 2, with B k 8.

Row 12: With B p 8, * with B p 2; rep from * 4 times more; with A p 2, with B p 9.
Rep Rows 9 through 12 eight times more; then rep Rows 9 and 10 once more. Work 8 rows with B in St st. Bind off.

Motif C (Make 5 with color A as background; make 4 with color B as background.)
With color A cast on 39 sts. Work 8 rows in St st.
Then follow Chart C as follows:

Row 9: With A k 7, * with B k 1, with A k 1; rep from * 12 times; with A k 6.

Row 10: With A p across.

Rows 11 & 13: With A k 6, with B k 27, with A k 6.

Row 12: With A p 6, * with B p 1, with A p 1; rep from * 12 times more; with B p 1, with A p 6.

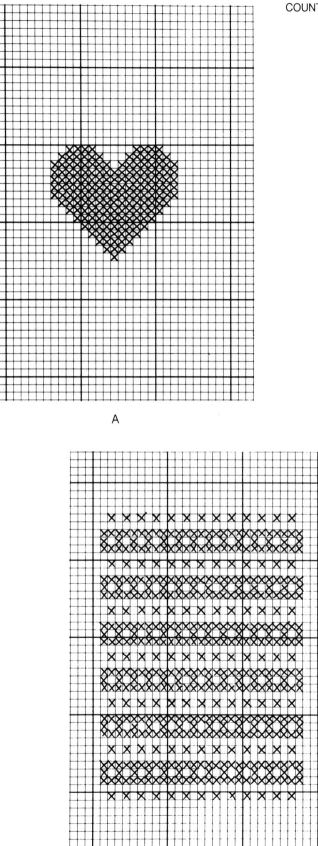

A

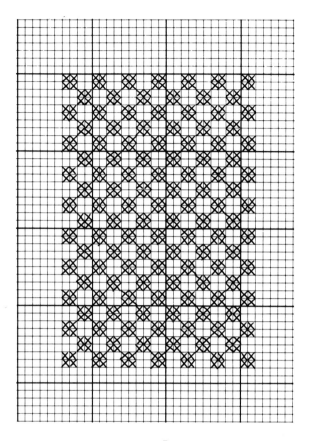

B

C

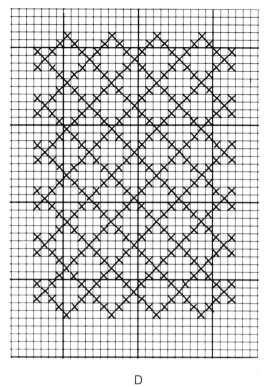

D

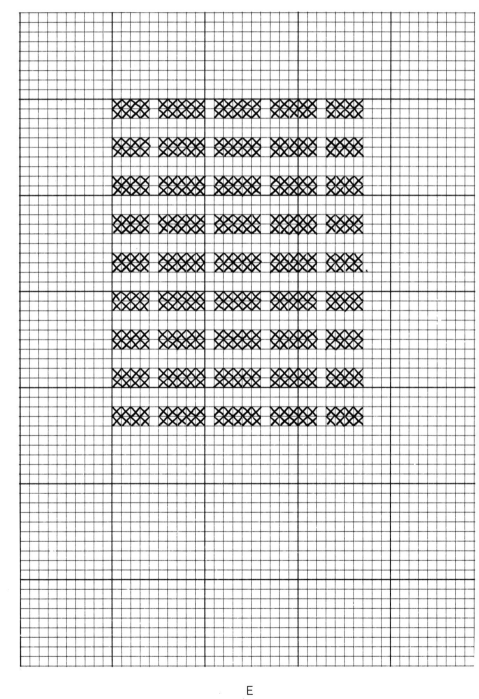

E

Row 14: With A p across.
Rep Rows 9 through 14 five times more.

Next Row: Rep Row 9.
Beginning with a purl row and using color A, work 9 rows in St st. Bind off.

Motif D (Make 4 with color B as background color and color A as contrast color; make 5 with color A as background and color B as contrast color.)
Using color B cast on 39 sts. Work 8 rows in St st. Then follow Chart D:

Row 9: With color B k 10, * with A k 1, with B k 5; rep from * 2 times more; with A k 1, with B k 10.

Row 10: With B p 9, * with A p 1, with B p 1, with A p 1, with B p 3; rep from * 3 times more; with B p 6.

Row 11: With B k 6, * with A k 1, with B k 1, with A k 1, with B k 3; rep from * 3 times more; with A k 1, with B k 1, with A k 1, with B k 6.

Row 12: With B p 7, * with A p 1, with B p 5; rep from * 3 times more; with A p 1, with B p 7.

Row 13: With B k 6, * with A k 1, with B k 1, with A k 1, with B k 3; rep from * 3 times more; with A k 1, with B k 1, with A k 1, with B k 6.

Row 14: With B p 9, * with A p 1, with B p 1, with A p 1, with B p 3; rep from * 2 times more; with A p 1, with B p 1, with A p 1, with B p 9.
Rep Rows 9 through 14 five times more.

Next Row: Rep Row 9.
With B and beginning with a purl row, work 9 rows in St st. Bind off.

Motif E (Make 4 with color A as background and color B as contrast color; make 6 with color B as background and color A as contrast color.)
With color A cast on 39 sts. Work 8 rows in St st. Then follow Chart E as follows:

Row 9: With A k 6, drop A, with B k 4, sl 1 as to p, * with B k 5, sl 1 as to p; rep from * 2 times more; with B k 4, join another ball of A and k 6.

Row 10: With A p 6, with B k 4, yarn forward, sl 1, yarn back, * with B k 5, yarn forward, sl 1, yarn back; rep from * 2 times more; with B k 4, with A p 6.

Row 11: With A only k 7, sl 1 as to p, * k 5, sl 1 as to p; rep from * 3 times more; k 7.

Row 12: With A only p across, slipping all sl sts of Row 11.
Rep Rows 9 through 12 eight times more; then rep Rows 9 and 10 once more. With A, work 8 rows in St st. Bind off.

Border Section (Make 4.)
With A cast on 5 sts.

Row 1: K 5.

Row 2: P 5.

Row 3 & every odd-numbered row through 19: K 1, inc 1 in next st, k across to last 2 sts, inc 1, k 1.

Row 4 & every even-numbered row through Row 20: P across to center 5 sts; k 2, p 1, k 2; p across rem sts.

Row 21: Knit. Rep Rows 20 and 21 for 63 inches, end with a p row.

Next Row (dec row): K 1, sl 1, k 1, psso, k 17, k 2 tog, k 1.
Then continue in pat dec 1 st at each end of k row in same way until 5 sts rem. Bind off.

TO FINISH

Block motifs on wrong side with damp cloth and warm iron. Follow the diagram for placement and join motifs. Sew ends of the border sections tog; then fold in half and sew in place along outer edge.

COUNTRY HEARTS ASSEMBLY DIAGRAM

E	A ♥	B	C	D	E	A ♥
A ♥	B	C	D	E	A ♥	B
B	C	D	E	A ♥	B	C
C	D	E	A ♥	B	C	D
D	E	A ♥	B	C	D	E
E	A ♥	B	C	D	E	A ♥
A ♥	B	C	D	E	A ♥	B

Country Hearts Pillow

*M*ake a matching pillow or two to go with the hearts afghan. This oblong shape measures 13 × 16 inches.

MATERIALS: Phildar Quality Leader knitting worsted (3.5 oz./100 gram balls) 2 balls of gray, 1 ball of red.

Knitting Needles: #6 (4.25 mm) or size needed for correct gauge. Poly-Fil® stuffing.

GAUGE: Stockinette st: 19 sts = 4 inches; 27 rows = 4 inches.

Stockinette Stitch (St st): K 1 row. P 1 row. Rep 2 rows for pat. Embroider with duplicate stitch.

DIRECTIONS
With A cast on 68 sts. Work in St st for 78 rows (13 inches). Bind off.

TO FINISH
Follow Chart A and embroider 3 hearts with C, placing point of first heart on 20th st of 12th row, point of 2nd heart on 20th st of 32nd row, and point of 3rd heart on 20th st of 52nd row. Cut 2 pieces of fabric the size of knit piece plus ½ inch on all edges for seams. Pin knit piece to one fabric piece; place other fabric piece over knit piece, right sides together. Sew, leaving 6-inch opening. Turn and stuff. Sew opening closed.

VARIATION NO. 1

A – navy blue
B – white
C – red

VARIATION NO. 2

A – deep red
B and C – white

TEXTURED KNIT

*M*y mother, Ruth Linsley, calls this her "left-over yarn afghan" because you can use the leftover yarns from other projects. Almost any color combination looks good. The different textures of each panel make this an interesting lap throw. It is 33 × 37 inches, which makes the perfect cover-up to keep on the sofa for chilly evenings.

MATERIALS: Phildar Prognostic knitting worsted (1.75 oz./50 gram skeins) — 5 skeins color A (gray), 3 skeins each of colors B (ecru) and C (red); 2 skeins color D (navy blue).

Knitting Needles: #8 (5mm) or size needed for correct gauge; #7 (4.5 mm) dp cable needle.

Crochet Hook: #6/G (4.5 mm).
Large-eye yarn needle.

GAUGE: 5 stockinette sts = 1 inch; 6 rows = 1 inch.

DIRECTIONS

NOTE: Bottom and top borders of all strips — k 8 rows. Side borders (SB) of all strips — k 1, p 1, k 1, p 1 (seed stitch) at beginning and end of all rows.

Pattern: Bottom and top borders of all strips knit 8 rows.

Side Border (SB) of all strips k 1, p 1, k 1, p 1 (seed stitch) at the beginning and end of every row.

Strip 1 (Diagonal Strips)

Using color A (gray), cast on 32 sts. Knit first 8 rows.

Pattern = 8 rows.

Row 1: SB (k 1, p 1, k 1, p 1), *k 4, p 4, rep from * across row to last 4 sts; SB (k 1, p 1, k 1, p 1).

Row 2: SB; k 3, p 4, k 4, p 4, k 4, p 4, k 1; SB.

Row 3: SB; p 2, k 4, p 4, k 4, p 4, k 4, p 2, SB.

Row 4: SB; k 1, p 4, k 4, p 4, k 4, p 4, k 3, SB.

Row 5: SB; p 4, k 4, across row to last 4 sts, SB.

Row 6: SB; p 3, k 4, p 4, k 4, p 4, k 4, p 1, SB.

Row 7: SB; k 2, p 4, k 4, p 4, k 4, p 4, k 2, SB.

Row 8: SB; p 1, k 4, p 4, k 4, p 4, p 3, SB.

Repeat pattern until strip measures approximately 35½ inches, then knit 8 border rows for 37-inch strip. Bind off.

Strip 2 (squares)

Using color B (ecru), cast on 30 sts. Knit first 8 rows for bottom border.

Pattern = 10 rows.

Row 1: SB; k across, SB.

Row 2: SB; p across, SB.

Row 3: SB; k 2, k 1, p 1 for 8 sts, k 2, k 1, p 1 for 8 sts, k 2, SB.

Row 4: SB; p 2, k 1, p 1 for 8 sts, p 2, k 1, p 1 for 8 sts, p 2, SB.

Row 5: Repeat Row 3.

Row 6: Repeat Row 4.

Row 7: Repeat Row 3.

Row 8: Repeat Row 4.

Row 9: Repeat Row 1.

Row 10: Repeat Row 2.

Repeat pattern until strip measures approximately 35½ inches, then knit 8 border rows for 37-inch strip. Bind off.

Strip 3 (cable)
Using color D (navy blue), cast on 26 sts. Knit first 8 rows for bottom border.

Pattern = 8 rows.

Row 1: SB; k 4, p 2, k 6, p 2, k 4, SB.

Row 2: SB; p 4, k 2, p 6, k 2, p 4, SB.

Row 3: Repeat Row 1.

Row 4: Repeat Row 2.

Start of pattern.

Row 5: SB; k 4, p 2, slip next 3 sts to cable needle and hold in front. K next 3 sts, slide the 3 sts on the cable needle to right and knit these 3 sts. P 2, k 4, SB.

Row 6: Repeat Row 2.

Row 7: Repeat Row 1.

Rows 8 through 12: Repeat Rows 2 and 1 twice and then Row 2 again. This completes the cable pattern.

Repeat Rows 5 through 12 until the strip measures 35½ inches. Then knit 8 border rows. Bind off.

Strip 4 (checkered pattern)
Using color C (red), cast on 32 sts. Knit 8 rows for bottom border.

Pattern = 16 rows.

Row 1: SB; k 8, p 8, k 8, SB.

Row 2: SB; p 8, k 8, p 8, SB.

Repeat Rows 1 and 2 until you have 8 rows.

Row 9: SB; p 8, k 8, p 8, SB.

Row 10: SB; k 8, p 8, k 8, SB.

Repeat Row 9 and 10 through Row 16.

Repeat Rows 1 through 16 until strip measures approximately 35½ inches. Knit 8 border rows to complete the 37-inch strip.

Strip 5 (zigzag pattern)
Using color A (gray), cast on 32 sts. Knit 8 rows for bottom border.

Pattern = 48 rows.

Row 1: SB; k 24; SB.

Row 2: SB; p 23, k 1; SB.

Row 3: SB; p 2, k 22; SB.

Row 4: SB; p 21, k 3; SB.

Row 5: SB; p 4, k 20; SB.

Row 6: SB; p 19, k 5; SB.

Row 7: SB; p 6, k 18; SB.

Row 8: SB; p 17, k 7; SB.

Row 9: SB; p 18, k 16; SB.

Row 10: SB; p 15, k 9; SB.

Row 11: SB; p 10, k 14; SB.

Row 12: SB; p 13, k 11; SB.

Row 13: SB; p 12, k 12; SB.

Row 14: SB; p 11, k 14; SB.

Row 15: SB; p 14, k 10; SB.

Row 16: SB; p 9, k 15; SB.

Row 17: SB; p 16, k 8; SB.

Row 18: SB; p 7, k 17; SB.

Row 19: SB; p 18, k 6; SB.

Row 20: SB; p 5, k 19; SB.

Row 21: SB; p 20, k 4; SB.

Row 22: SB; p 3, k 21; SB.

Row 23: SB; p 22, k 2; SB.

Row 24: SB; p 1, k 23; SB.

Row 25: SB; p 24; SB.

Row 26: SB; p 1, k 23; SB.

Row 27: SB; p 22, k 2; SB.

Row 28: SB; p 3, k 21; SB.

Row 29: SB; p 20, k 4; SB.

Row 30: SB; p 5, k 19; SB.

Row 31: SB; p 18, k 6; SB.

Row 32: SB; p 7, k 17; SB.

Row 33: SB; p 16, k 8; SB.

Row 34: SB; p 9, k 15; SB.

Row 35: SB; p 14, k 10; SB.

Row 36: SB; p 11, k 13; SB.

Row 37: SB; p 12, k 12; SB.

Row 38: SB; p 13, k 11; SB.

Row 39: SB; p 10, k 14; SB.

Row 40: SB; p 15, k 9; SB.

Row 41: SB; p 8, k 16; SB.

Row 42: SB; p 17, k 7; SB.

Row 43: SB; p 6, k 18; SB.

Row 44: SB; p 19, k 5; SB.

Row 45: SB; p 4, k 20; SB.

Row 46: SB; p 21, k 3; SB.

Row 47: SB; p 2, k 22; SB.

Row 48: SB; p 23, k 1; SB.

Repeat from Row 1 until strip measures approximately 35½ inches. Knit 8 rows for top border. Bind off.

TO FINISH

Using yarn needle and color gray yarn, sew strips together from wrong side in order of the strip numbers (1 through 5).

Edging

Rnd 1: Using crochet hook and color C (red), dc in each stitch all around, with 2 dc in each st at each corner.

Rnd 2: Using color B (ecru), sc all around.

Rnd 3: Using color D (navy blue), sc all around. 5 dc in each st at corners.

Scallop Edging

Using crochet hook and color C (red), * 2 sc, 1 dc in each of next 5 sts. Repeat from* all around. At corners, 2 dc in each st. (10 dc).

Blocking

See page 19 for blocking details.

VARIATION NO. 1

A – brown
A and C – sienna
D – ochre

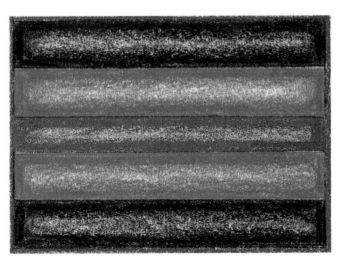

VARIATION NO. 2

A – navy blue
B and C – bright blue
D – red

LACE GRANNY

*T*his delicate afghan is crocheted in a deep wine color and measures 48 × 59 inches. The yarn is 100% superwool, which means it is machine washable and dryable just like acrylic. The stitches give it an interesting texture, and it's the perfect portable project.

MATERIALS: Lane Borgosesia "Knitaly" (3.5 oz./100 gram skein)—16 skeins wine.

Crochet Hook: 5/F (4 mm) or size needed for correct gauge.

GAUGE: 4 dc = 1 inch.

DIRECTIONS

Each square measures approximately 11 inches.

Berry Stitch: Work 5 dc in same st or sp, remove hook; insert hook in first dc and pull dropped lp through first dc.

Square (Make 20.)
Ch 8, join with sl st to form a ring.

Rnd 1: Ch 3, 3 dc in ring, ch 5, (4 dc in ring, ch 5) 3 times. Join with sl st in 3rd ch of starting ch 3.

Rnd 2: Ch 3, work 1 dc in each of next 3 dc, work * 2 dc in next ch-5 lp; (dc, ch 5, dc) in 3rd ch of same ch-5 lp (corner made); 2 dc in same ch-5 lp, 1 dc in each of next 4 dc. Repeat from * 2 times, end 2 dc in last ch-5 lp, corner (see above), 2 dc in same ch-5 lp, corner, 2 dc in same ch-5 lp, 1 dc in each of next 3 dc. Join with sl st in 3rd ch of starting ch 3.

Rnd 3: Ch 3, work 1 dc in each of next 6 dc, * 2 dc in next ch-5 lp, corner (see Rnd 2), 2 dc in same ch-5 lp, 1 dc in each of next 10 dc. Repeat from * 2 times, end 2 dc in last ch-5 lp, corner, 2 dc in same ch-5 lp, 1 dc in each of next 3 dc. Join with sl st in 3rd ch of starting ch 3.

Rnd 4: Ch 3, 1 dc in each of next 6 dc, * ch 2, sk 2 dc, 1 dc in next dc, ch 2, corner, ch 2, 1 dc in next dc, ch 2, sk 2 dc, 1 dc in each of next 10 dc. Repeat from * 2 times, end ch 2, sk 2 dc, 1 dc in next dc, ch 2, corner, ch 2, 1 dc in next dc, ch 2, sk 2 dc, 1 dc in each of next 3 dc. Join with sl st in 3rd ch of starting ch 3.

Rnd 5: Ch 3, 1 dc in each of next 3 dc, * ch 2, sk 2 dc, 1 dc in next dc, ch 2, 1 dc in next dc, 2 dc in next ch-2 sp, 1 dc in next dc, 2 dc in next ch-5 lp, corner, 2 dc in same ch-5 lp, 1 dc in next dc, 2 dc in next ch-2 sp, 1 dc in next dc, ch 2, 1 dc in next dc, ch 2, sk 2 dc, 1 dc in each of next 4 dc. Repeat from * 2 times, end ch 2, sk 2 dc, 1 dc in next dc, ch 2, 1 dc in next dc, 2 dc in next ch-2 sp, 1 dc in next dc, 2 dc in next ch-5 lp, corner, 2 dc in same ch-5 lp, 1 dc in next dc, 2 dc in next ch-2 sp, 1 dc in next dc, ch 2, 1 dc in next dc, ch 2. Join with sl st in 3rd ch of starting ch 3.

Rnd 6: Ch 5, sk 2 dc, 1 dc in next dc, ch 2, 1 dc in next dc, * 1 berry in next ch-2 sp, 1 dc in same sp, (1 berry in next dc, 1 dc in next dc) 3 times, 1 berry in next dc, corner, (1 berry in next dc, 1 dc in next dc) 3 times, 1 berry in next dc, 1 dc in next ch-2 sp, 1 berry in same sp, 1 dc in next dc, ch 2 **, 1 dc in next dc, ch 2, sk 2 dc, 1 dc in next dc, ch 2, 1 dc in next dc. Repeat from * 2 times, then from * to ** once. Join with sl st in 3rd ch of starting ch 5.

Rnd 7: Ch 5, 1 dc in next dc, ch 2, 1 dc in next dc, * ch 2, sk 2 berries, 1 dc in next dc, (ch 2, 1 dc in next dc) 3 times, ch 2, corner, (ch 2, 1 dc in next dc) 4 times, ch 2, sk 2 berries, 1 dc in next dc, (ch 2 **, 1 dc in next dc) 3 times. Repeat from * 2 times, then from * to ** once. Join with sl st in 3rd ch of starting ch 5.

Rnd 8: Ch 5, 1 dc in next dc, (ch 2, 1 dc in next dc) 3 times, * (2 dc in next ch-2 sp, 1 dc in next dc) 3 times, corner, (1 dc in next dc, 2 dc in next ch-2 sp) 3 times, 1 dc in next dc **, (ch 2, 1 dc in next dc) 7 times. Repeat from * 2 times, then from * to ** once, end (ch 2, 1 dc in next dc) 2 times, ch 2. Join with sl st in 3rd ch of starting ch 5.

Rnd 9: Ch 5, 1 dc in next dc, (ch 2, 1 dc in next dc) twice, * 1 berry in next ch-2 sp, 1 dc in same sp, (1 berry in next dc, 1 dc in next dc) 5 times, 1 berry in next dc, corner (1 berry in next dc, 1 dc in next dc) 5 times, 1 berry in next dc, 1 dc in next ch-2 sp, 1 berry in same sp, 1 dc in next dc **, (ch 2, 1 dc in next dc) 5 times. Repeat from * 2 times, then from * to ** once, end ch 2, 1 dc in next dc, ch 2. Join with sl st in 3rd ch of starting ch 5. Fasten off.

TO FINISH

When each square is completed, it will have a ruffled appearance that needs to be blocked out, but this need not be done before joining. From right side, work 1 row sc around each square, working 7 sc in each ch-5 corner lp. Sew squares tog, 4 squares wide by 5 squares long, by overcasting from wrong side. After squares have been joined, block with a wet towel on the wrong side, pulling each square out to make the edges straight. Allow to dry flat. After dry, fluff up the berries which may have been flattened during blocking.

Edging: From right side, work 5 rnds sc around entire outside edge of afghan, working 3 sc in each corner.

Next Rnd: Working 3 sc in each corner, work 1 sc in each of next 3 sc, * 1 berry in next sc, 1 sc in each of next 3 sc. Repeat from * around. Work 5 more rnds of sc.

Final Rnd: Working from left to right, sc in each st around. Fasten off.

VARIATION NO. 1

Change materials to 8 skeins of dusty rose, 8 skeins of medium gray to create the pattern as shown.

VARIATION NO. 2

Change materials to 8 skeins of forest green, 8 skeins of medium brown to create the pattern shown.

Rainbow Ripple

A *ripple pattern has always been popular with crocheters. The pattern can vary depending on the color combinations used and the width of each ripple stripe. This colorful arrangement designed by Elizabeth Grace Linquist is especially pretty. It is a 14-color sequence repeated twice and is a favorite of its owner, Elizabeth's son Karl Lindquist, for whom she made it many years ago. This finished afghan is 48 × 75 inches.*

MATERIALS: Worsted weight (3.5 oz./100 gram skeins)—1 skein each of A (dark brown), B (medium brown), C (tan), D (wine), E (red), F (pink), G (forest green), H (olive green), I (light aqua green), J (dark orange), K (light orange), L (yellow), M (dark blue), N (light blue).

Crochet Hook: #5/F (4 mm) or size needed for correct gauge.

GAUGE: 14 sc = 2½ inches; 7 rows = 4 inches.

DIRECTIONS

The color sequence is as follows: A, B, C, D, E, F, G, H, I, J, K, L, M, N, N, M, L, K, J, I, H, G, F, E, D, C, B, A. Note that you will use 14 colors, beginning with A and ending with N. Then you will repeat the last color, N, and work back to A in the color sequence.

Using color A, ch 295, ch 2, and turn.

Row 1: Sc into 3rd ch from hook. * Sc into each of next 11 ch, skip 2, ch 1, sc into each of next 11 ch, 3 sc into next ch, repeat from * to end, but end with 2 sc in last ch instead of 3.

Row 2: Ch 1, sc into same place, * sc into each of next 11 sc, skip 2 sc, 1 sc into each of next 11 sc, 3 sc into next sc, rep from * to end, but end with 2 sc into second-from-last ch and 2 sc in last chain.

Rep Row 2 throughout, working 7 more rows in A, then 8 rows in each additional color (see color sequence) to end.

TO FINISH

Use one of the colors to sc an edging around the entire afghan.

VARIATION NO. 1

A, B, C, D – yellow, yellow-orange, tangerine, lemon yellow

E, F, G, H – Repeat sequence above

I, J, K, L – Repeat sequence above

M, N, O – yellow, yellow-orange, tangerine

VARIATION NO. 2

In this variation there are 15 colors rather than 14. The sequence is as follows: A, B, C, D, E, F, G, H, I, J, K, L, M, N, O, N, M, L, K, L, K, J, I, H, G, F, E, D, C, B, A. Color O is a strip of yellow that marks the center of the afghan. It is the only color that is not repeated.

A, B, C, D – 4 shades of blue from dark to light

E, F, G, H – 4 shades of red from maroon to pink

I, J, K, L – 4 shades of purple from deep purple to pale lavender

M, N – 2 shades of orange

O – yellow

PUPPY PAWS

*A*pproximately 50 × 60 inches, this adorable puppy afghan is an ample size to fit a full-size crib. It is made of acrylic and is washable. The puppy fills the center and paw prints create a border all around. The red-and-black color scheme is cheerful for any child's room, but you might like to use one of the alternate color combinations for a different look.

MATERIALS: Unger's Utopia 4-ply acrylic (3.5 oz./100 gram balls)— 9 balls of MC (white), 2 balls of A (red), 1 ball each of B (black), C (beige), D (blue).

Crochet Hook: #10/J (6 mm) or size needed for correct gauge.

GAUGE: 7 sc = 2 inches; 3 rows = 1 inch.

DIRECTIONS

Center Panel: (28 × 38 inches)
With MC (white), ch 98.

Row 1 First Half: Pull up a lp onto hook in each ch across. **Second Half:** Yo and pull through 1 lp, * yo and pull through 2 lps; rep from * across (1 lp).

Row 2 First Half: Pull up a lp in each st, inserting hook under the vertical bar (98 lps). **Second Half:** Same as second half of Row 1. Rep Row 2 for afghan st pat until piece measures 38 inches, end on second half of row.

Finishing Row: * Pull up a lp under vertical bar and through the lp on hook. Rep from * across. Fasten off.

Side Panels: (Make 2, 8 × 57 inches.)
With MC, ch 28. Work in afghan st pat until piece measures 57 inches. Fasten off.

End Panels: (Make 2, 8 × 31 inches.)
With MC, ch 28. Work in afghan st pat until piece measures 31 inches. Fasten off.
Following Chart 1, embroider design in cross-stitch on center panel.

Center Panel Corner

Rnd 1: From right side, join A in a corner, sc evenly around entire outer edge, having 3 sc in each corner and same number of sc on opposite edges, end with 2 sc in same place as first sc. Join.

Rnd 2: Ch 1, sc in joining, * ch 1, sk 1 sc, sc in next sc*. Rep from * to * to next corner st, in corner sc work sc, ch 1, and sc. Rep from * to * to next corner and continue in this way around. Join.

Rnds 3 through 5: Ch 1, * sc in next ch sp, ch 1, sk next sc. Rep from * around with sc, ch 1, and sc in each corner ch sp.

TO FINISH

Sew end panels to each narrow edge of center panel. Then sew side panels to center and end panels. Following Chart 2, use color B to embroider in cross-stitch 4 paw prints evenly spaced along each end panel and 7 prints spaced along each side panel, all 2 sts from each side.

Outer Edging

Rnd 1: From right side, join color A in a corner, work 3 sc in same place, * ch 1, sk ¼ inch along edge, sc in next 3 sts or end of rows along edge. Rep from * around, having same number of sc groups on corresponding edges and 3 sc in each corner. Join with sl st in first sc.

Rnd 2: Ch 3, in corner sc work 2 dc and ch 3, 2 dc, dc in next sc, * ch 1, dc in next 3 sc. Rep from * to next corner, ch 1, dc in first sc of corner, 2 dc and ch 3, 2 dc in next sc, dc in next sc, ch 1, dc in next 3 sc, and continue around. End with ch 1. Join to top of beg ch.

Rnd 3: Ch 3, dc in next 2 dc, ch 1. In corner sp work 2 dc, ch 3, 2 dc, * ch 1, dc in next 3 dc. Rep from * to next corner sp, work corner sp as before and continue around. Join to beg ch.

Rnd 4: Ch 1, sc in joining and in each dc around, skipping ch-1 sps and having 3 sc in each corner sp. Join.

Rnd 5: Ch 1, sc in each sc around, having 3 sc in each corner sc. Join. Fasten off.

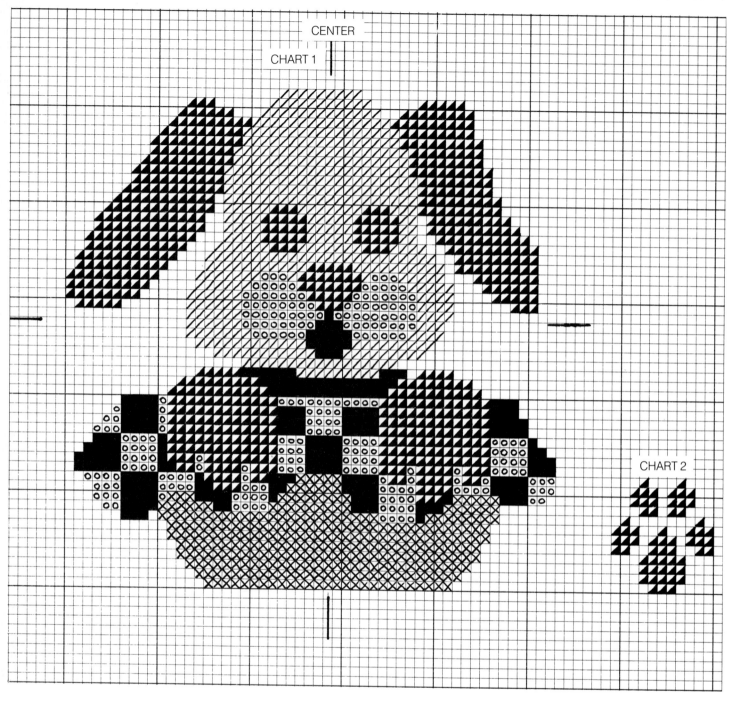

CENTER

CHART 1

CHART 2

PUPPY PAWS CHART

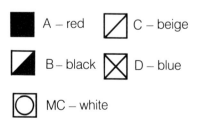

A – red   C – beige

B – black   D – blue

MC – white

126

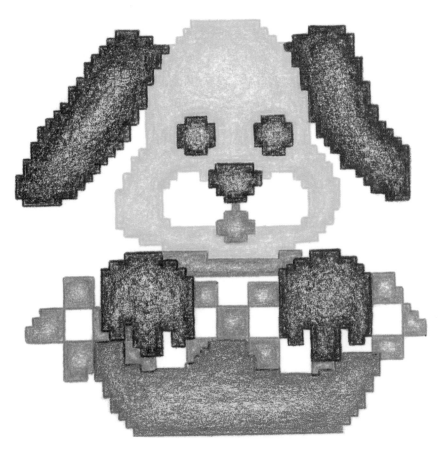

VARIATION NO. 1

A – blue
B – brown
C – deep yellow
D – red
MC – white
Puppy's tongue – blue

VARIATION NO. 2

A – bright green
B – brown
C – beige
D – dark green
MC – white
Puppy's tongue – red

127

CARNIVAL STRIPE

*T*his afghan was designed by Tillie Sparrow for Crystal Palace Yarns. It takes only 11 balls of 100% wool and is easy to crochet. The stripes of blue, lavender, and lilac are offset by white, but you might like to use another equally pretty color combination. The finished size is 57 × 70 inches.

MATERIALS: Crystal Palace Carnival wool (3.5 oz./100 gram balls)—5 balls of white (MC); 2 balls each of A (lavender), B (blue), C (lilac).

Crochet Hook: #13/M (0.6 mm) or size needed for correct gauge.

GAUGE: 14 (dc) sts = 4 inches.

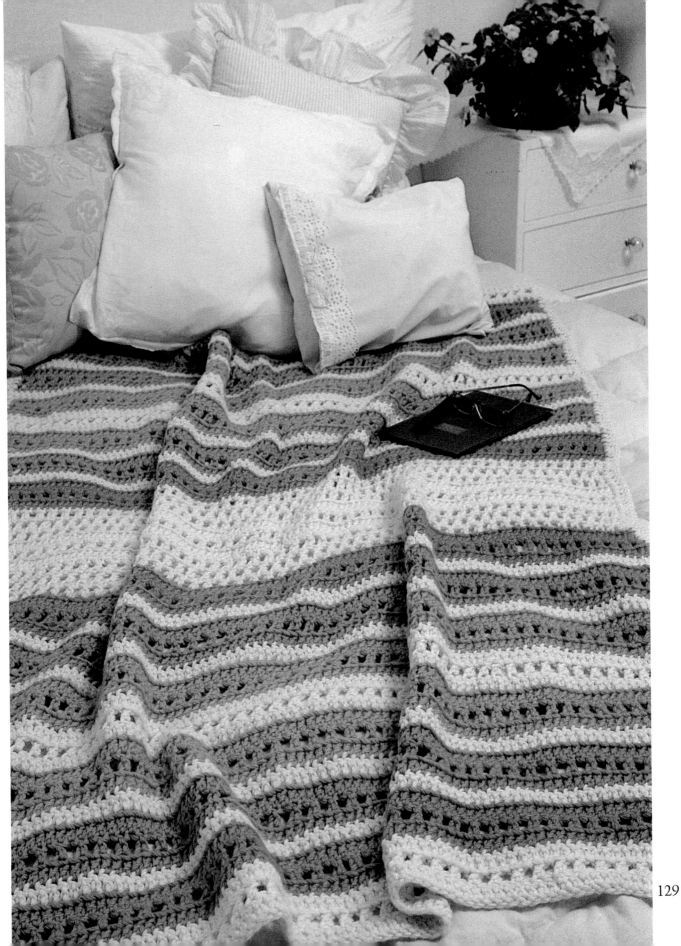

DIRECTIONS

With white (MC), ch 114.

Row 1: Dc in 3rd ch from hook, dc in each ch across (112 dc).

Row 2: Ch 4, * skip one dc, dc in next dc *, repeat from * to * across.

Row 3: Ch 3, dc across row.

Rows 4 through 6: Change to color A. Repeat Rows 1 through 3.

Row 7: Change to MC and ch 3, dc across.

Rows 8 through 10: Change to B and repeat Rows 1 through 3.

Row 11: Change to MC and ch 3, dc across.

Rows 12 through 14: Change to C and repeat Rows 1 through 3.

Rows 15 through 17: Change to MC and repeat Rows 1 through 3.

Rows 18 through 20: Change to C and repeat Rows 1 through 3.

Row 21: Change to MC and ch 3, dc across.

Rows 22 through 24: Change to B and repeat Rows 1 through 3.

Row 25: Change to MC, ch 3, and dc across.

Rows 26 through 28: Change to A and repeat Rows 1 through 3.

Row 29: Change to MC and ch 4, sk 1 dc, * dc in next dc, ch 1, sk 1 dc *, repeat bet *s across.

Row 30: Ch 4, dc in ch 1, * ch 1, sk 1 dc, dc in ch 1*, repeat bet *s across ending with dc in last ch.

Row 31: Repeat Row 29.

Row 32: Ch 3, dc across row.

Row 33: Repeat Row 29.

Row 34: Repeat Row 30.

Row 35 through 37: Repeat Rows 29 through 31.

Rows 38 through 62: Repeat Rows 4 through 28 as above.

Rows 63 through 65: Change to MC and repeat Rows 1 through 3.

TO FINISH

With MC, work one row of dc along each side edge of the entire afghan.

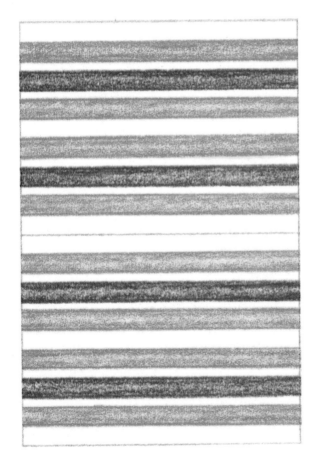

VARIATION NO. 1

MC – white
A and C – peach
B – green

VARIATION NO. 2

MC – black
A and C – violet
B – olive green

Easy Knit

W*hile this lovely afghan might look difficult to knit, it is actually quite easy to do. It's a portable project because each section is made in strips and then stitched together when finished. The variety of stitches gives it texture and interest.*

My mother, Ruth Linsley, designed this afghan in red, light gray, and dark gray worsted weight yarn. But as you can see from the sketches, other color combinations make pretty alternatives. The finished project is approximately 47 × 51 inches. It is completely washable.

MATERIALS: Phildar's Pegase classic worsted (80% acrylic/20% wool; 1.75 oz./50 gram skeins)—11 skeins A (light gray), 5 skeins B (red), 3 skeins C (dark gray).

Knitting Needles: #8 (5 mm) or size needed for correct gauge; #7 (4.5 mm) dp cable needle.

Crochet Hook: #6/G (4.5 mm).
Large-eye yarn needle.

GAUGE: 5 sts = 1 inch; 6 rows = 1 inch.

DIRECTIONS

NOTE: Bottom and top borders on all strips—knit 10 rows. In the pattern directions, right-side border (RSB) means k 1, p 1, k 1, p 1. Left-side border (LSB) means p 1, k 1, p 1, k 1.

Strip 1: Narrow Triangles
Using color A and #8 needles, cast on 29 stitches.
Knit 10 border rows.

Row 1: RSB (k 1, p 1, k 1, p 1), k 21, LSB (p 1, k 1, p 1, k 1).

Row 2: RSB, p 20, k 1, LSB.

Row 3: RSB, p 2, k 19, LSB.

Row 4: RSB, p 18, k 3, LSB.

Row 5: RSB, p 4, k 17, LSB.

Row 6: RSB, p 16, k 5, LSB.

Row 7: RSB, p 6, k 15, LSB.

Row 8: RSB, p 14, k 7, LSB.

Row 9: RSB, p 8, k 13, LSB.

Row 10: RSB, p 12, k 9, LSB.

Row 11: RSB, p 10, k 11, LSB.

Row 12: RSB, p 10, k 11, LSB.

Row 13: RSB, p12, k 9, LSB.

Row 14: RSB, p 8, k 13, LSB.

Row 15: RSB, p 14, k 7, LSB.

Row 16: RSB, p 6, k 15, LSB.

Row 17: RSB, p 16, k 5, LSB.

Row 18: RSB, p 4, k 17, LSB.

Row 19: RSB, p 18, k 3, LSB.

Row 20: RSB, p 2, k 19, LSB.

Row 21: RSB, p 20, k 1, LSB.

Row 22: RSB, p 21, LSB.

Repeat pattern Rows 1 through 22 until strip measures 49 inches. Add 10 knit rows for top border. Bind off.

Strip 2: Checkerboard
With color B, cast on 29 stitches. Knit 10 rows for the bottom border.

Row 1: RSB, k 7, p 7, k 7, LSB.

Row 2: RSB, p 7, k 7, p 7, LSB.

Rows 3 through 8: Repeat last 2 rows 3 times.

Row 9: RSB, p 7, k 7, p 7, LSB.

Row 10: RSB, k 7, p 7, k 7, LSB.

Rows 11 through 16: Repeat Rows 9 and 10 three times.
Repeat Rows 1 through 16 until strip measures 49 inches. Knit 10 rows for top border. Bind off.

Strip 3: Cable
With color A, cast on 34 stitches. Knit 10 rows for the bottom border.

Row 1: RSB, k 7, p 3, k 6, p 3, k 7, LSB.

Row 2: RSB, p 7, k 3, p 6, k 3, p 7, LSB.

Row 3: Repeat Row 1.

Row 4: Repeat Row 2.

Row 5 (start of pattern): RSB, k 7, p 3, slip next 3 sts to cable needle and hold in front. K next 3 sts, slide the 3 sts on the cable needle to right and knit these 3 sts. P 3, k 7, LSB.

Row 6: Repeat Row 2.

Row 7: Repeat Row 1.

Rows 8 through 12: Repeat Rows 2 and 1 twice and then Row 2 again. This completes the cable pattern.
Repeat Rows 5 through 12 until strip measures 49 inches. Knit 10 rows for top border. Bind off.

Strip 4: Diamonds and Triangles
Using color C, cast on 39 stitches. Knit 10 border rows. Note that the RSB and LSB for this strip consist of 8 stitches instead of 4.

Row 1: K 1, p 1 for 8 sts (RSB); k 23; k 1, p 1 for 8 sts (LSB).

Row 2: RSB, k 1, p 21, k 1, LSB.

Row 3: RSB, p 2, k 19, p 2, LSB.

Row 4: RSB, k 3, p 17, k 3, LSB.

Row 5: RSB, p 4, k 15, p 4, LSB.

Row 6: RSB, k 5, p 13, k 5, LSB.

Row 7: RSB, p 6, k 11, p 6, LSB.

Row 8: RSB, k 7, p 9, k 7, LSB.

Row 9: RSB, p 8, k 7, p 8, LSB.

Row 10: RSB, k 9, p 5, k 9, LSB.

Row 11: RSB, p 10, k 3, p 10, LSB.

Row 12: RSB, k 11, p 1, k 11, LSB.

Repeat Row 11 and every row back to Row 1. Repeat Row 2 and continue to Row 12. Repeat Row 11 and continue back to Row 1. Continue in this manner until strip measures 49 inches.

Strip 5: Diagonal Stripes
Using color A, cast on 34 stitches. Knit 10 border rows.

Row 1: RSB, k 6, p 6, k 6, p 6, k 2, LSB.

Row 2: RSB, p 1, k 6, p 6, k 6, p 6, k 1, LSB.

Row 3: RSB, p 2, k 6, p 6, k 6, p 6, LSB.

Row 4: RSB, k 5, p 6, k 6, p 6, k 3, LSB.

Row 5: RSB, p 4, k 6, p 6, k 6, p 4, LSB.

Row 6: RSB, k 3, p 6, k 6, p 6, k 5, LSB.

Row 7: RSB, p 6, k 6, p 6, k 6, p 2, LSB.

Row 8: RSB, k 1, p 6, k 6, p 6, k 6, p 1, LSB.

Row 9: RSB, k 2, p 6, k 6, p 6, k 6, LSB.

Row 10: RSB, p 5, k 6, p 6, k 6, p 3, LSB.

Row 11: RSB, k 4, p 6, k 6, p 6, k 4, LSB.

Row 12: RSB, p 3, k 6, p 6, k 6, p 5, LSB.
Repeat Rows 1 through 12 until strip measures 49 inches. Knit 10 top border rows.

Strip 6: Crisscross
Using color B, cast on 29 sts. Knit 10 border rows.

Row 1: RSB, p 2, k 17, p 2, LSB.

Row 2: RSB, p 1, k 2, p 15, k 2, p 1, LSB.

Row 3: RSB, k 2, p 2, k 13, p 2, k 2, LSB.

Row 4: RSB, p 3, k 2, p 11, k 2, p 3, LSB.

Row 5: RSB, k 4, p 2, k 9, p 2, k 4, LSB.

Row 6: RSB, p 5, k 2, p 7, k 2, p 5, LSB.

Row 7: RSB, k 6, p 2, k 5, p 2, k 6, LSB.

Row 8: RSB, p 7, k 2, p 3, k 2, p 7, LSB.

Row 9: RSB, k 8, p 2, k 1, p 2, k 8, LSB.

Row 10: RSB, p 9, k 3, p 9, LSB.

Row 11: RSB, k 9, p 3, k 9, LSB.

Row 12: RSB, p 8, k 2, p 1, k 2, p 8, LSB.

Row 13: RSB, k 7, p 2, k 3, p 2, k 7, LSB.

Row 14: RSB, p 6, k 2, p 5, k 2, p 6, LSB.

Row 15: RSB, k 5, p 2, k 7, p 2, k 5, LSB.

Row 16: RSB, p 4, k 2, p 9, k 2, p 4, LSB.

Row 17: RSB, k 3, p 2, k 11, p 2, k 3, LSB.

Row 18: RSB, p 2, k 2, p 13, k 2, p 2, LSB.

Row 19: RSB, k 1, p 2, k 15, p 2, k 1, LSB.

Row 20: RSB, k 2, p 17, k 2, LSB.

Row 21: RSB, k 21, LSB.

Rows 22 through 30: RSB, k 21, LSB.

Repeat pattern Row 1 through Row 30 until strip measures 49 inches. Knit 10 rows for top border. Bind off.

Strip 7: Wide Triangles
Using color A, cast on 29 stitches. Knit 10 rows for bottom border.

Row 1: RSB, k 21, LSB.

Row 2: RSB, p 20, k 1, LSB.

Row 3: RSB, p 2, k 19, LSB.

Row 4: RSB, p 18, k 3, LSB.

Row 5: RSB, p 4, k 17, LSB.

Row 6: RSB, p 16, k 5, LSB.

Row 7: RSB, p 6, k 15, LSB.

Row 8: RSB, p 14, k 7, LSB.

Row 9: RSB, p 8, k 13, LSB.

Row 10: RSB, p 12, k 9, LSB.

Row 11: RSB, p 10, k 11, LSB.

Row 12: RSB, p 10, k 11, LSB.

Row 13: RSB, p 12, k 9, LSB.

Row 14: RSB, p 8, k 13, LSB.

Row 15: RSB, p 14, k 7, LSB.

Row 16: RSB, p 6, k 15, LSB.

Row 17: RSB, p 16, k 5, LSB.

Row 18: RSB, p 4, k 17, LSB.

Row 19: RSB, p 18, k 3, LSB.

Row 20: RSB, p 2, k 19, LSB.

Row 21: RSB, p 20, k 1, LSB.

Row 22: RSB, k 21, LSB.

Rows 23 through 42: Repeat backwards from Row 21 to Row 2. Then starting with Row 1, repeat the pattern until the strip measures 49 inches. Knit 10 top border rows. Bind off.

TO FINISH

Using the yarn needle and yarn color A, sew the strips together in order knitted on the wrong side with an overcast stitch. Using the crochet hook and yarn color B, sc all around the afghan.

To Make a Scalloped Edge: Using color A and crochet hook, * sc in next 3 sts, 3 dc. Repeat from * all around.

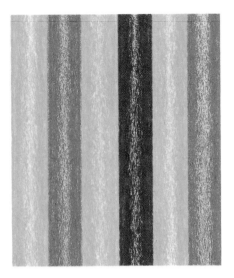

VARIATION NO. 1

A – yellow
B – orange
C – brown

VARIATION NO. 2

A – turquoise
B – dark turquoise
C – violet

FLOWERING GRANNIES

*T*his is a nice pattern for a two-tone afghan. It works with almost any color combination, and the afghan is a good size for a lap throw. The finished size is 42 × 42 inches.

MATERIALS: Phildar's Leader knitting worsted (3.5 oz./100 gram balls)—4 balls each of white and deep blue.

Crochet Hook: #8/H (5mm) or size needed for gauge.
Tapestry needle.

GAUGE: 1 rnd = 1 inch; 1 granny square = 5½ inches.

DIRECTIONS

Make 18 white squares with blue centers and 18 blue squares with white centers for a total of 36 squares.
With one color, ch 4 and join with sl st to form ring.

Rnd 1: Continuing with same color, ch 3; working over yarn end, 2 dc in ring, (ch 2, 3 dc in ring) 3 times. Ch 2, join with sl st in beg ch 3. Finish off.

Rnd 2: Without turning, join second color with sl st in any ch-2 sp, ch 3, (2 dc, ch 2, 3 dc) in same sp as joining. You have made the first corner. *(3 dc, ch 2, 3 dc) in next ch-2 sp (corner made); ch 1. Rep from * twice more. Join with a sl st in beg ch 3.

Rnd 3: Do not turn, sl st in any ch-2 corner sp; ch 3, (2 dc, ch 2, 3 dc) in same sp; *3 dc, ch 1 between next 2 grps of 3 dc for side, ch 1, (3 dc, ch 2, 3 dc) in next corner sp. Rep from * twice more, 3 dc bet next 2 grps of 3 dc for last side; ch 1, join with sl st in beg ch 3. Do not finish off.

Rnd 4: Do not turn; sl st in each of next 2 dc and into corner sp; ** ch 3, (2 dc, ch 2, 3 dc) in same sp; * 3 dc, ch 1 bet each pair of 3-dc grps along side, ch 1 (3 dc, ch 2, 3 dc) in next corner sp; rep from * twice more. 3 dc bet each pair of 3-dc grps along last side; ch 1, join with sl st in top of beg ch 3. Finish off**.

Rnd 5: Do not turn; continuing with same color, sl st in any corner sp. Work as for Rnd 4 from ** to **.

Rnd 6: Rep Rnd 5. Weave all ends into back of work.

TO FINISH

Beginning with a white square and alternating colors, arrange 6 squares to make a row. Lay out 6 rows in this way. With right sides together and matching sts on both squares, sew together with an overcast st in *outer lps only* across side. Begin and end with one corner st. Join squares in rows; then join rows as you did the squares.

Border

With right sides facing, join blue color yarn with sl st in any corner sp of afghan.

Rnd 1: Ch 3, (2 dc, ch 2, 3 dc) in any sp as joining along each side edge, work 3 dc bet each pair of 3-dc grps, and in each corner sp of squares on each side of joinings, and in each rem corner sp of the afghan. Work (3 dc, ch 2, 3dc), join with sl st in top of beg ch 3. Fasten off.

Rnd 2: Work in same manner as squares, 3 dc bet each pair of 3-dc grps along sides, ch 1, and (3 dc, ch 2, 3 dc) in each corner sp. Fasten off. Weave loose ends of yarn under back of afghan.

VARIATION NO. 1

Make 18 navy blue squares with red centers and 18 red squares with navy blue centers.

VARIATION NO. 2

Make 18 pink squares with gray centers and 18 gray squares with pink centers.

Sleeping Bunnies

Your favorite child will be delighted with the sleeping bunnies that border this 37 × 40-inch afghan, which is a good size to fit a full crib. As you can see, our baby model, Andrew, is happy to have his blanket along for picnicking. If the afghan is for a baby girl, make the bunnies from pink yarn and use gray for the tails, as shown on one of the sketches. Made from acrylic yarn, it is completely washable.

MATERIALS: Unger's Utopia 4-ply acrylic (3.5 oz./100 gram balls) —6 balls of color A (white); 1 ball each of color B (gray), color C (pink), color D (blue).

Crochet Hook: #10/J (6 mm) or size needed for correct gauge. Yarn needle.

GAUGE: 3 sc = 1 inch; 7 rows = 2 inches.

DIRECTIONS

Plain Motif (Make 6.)
With A, ch 40. **Foundation Row:** Sc in 2nd ch from hook, * ch 1, sk 1 ch, sc in next ch; rep from * across, end with sc in last 2 ch (20 sc and 18 sps). Ch 1 and turn.

Row 1: Sc in first sc, * ch 1, sk next sc, sc in next ch sp; rep from * across, end with sc in last ch sp, sc in last sc. Ch 1 and turn. Rep Row 1 for pat until piece measures 10½ inches. Fasten off.

Bunny Motif (Make 6: 3 with C trim and 3 with D trim.)
With B, ch 34.

Row 1: Sc in 2nd ch from hook and in each ch (33 sc). Ch 1, turn.

Row 2: Sc in each sc across. Ch 1, turn.

Rows 3 through 39: Rep Row 2 to complete stitch pattern, and follow chart to top for color changes. Fasten off.

Head and Ear
With B, ch 2.

Row 1: Work 3 sc in 2nd ch from hook. Ch 1, turn at end of each row hereafter.

Row 2: Sc in each sc, inc 1 sc at each end (5 sc).

Row 3: Inc 1 sc in first sc, sc across (6 sc).

Row 4: Sc across.

Row 5: Rep Row 3 through 7 sc.

Row 6: Sc to last sc, inc in last sc (8 sc).

Rows 7 & 8: Sc across.

Row 9: Sc across, dec 1 sc at each end (6 sc).

Row 10: Sc to last 2 sc, dec 1 sc (5 sc).

Row 11: (Beg. Ear) Sc in 3 sc, inc in next sc (6 sc).

Rows 12 & 13: Rep Rows 6 and 7.

Rows 14 & 15: Sc across.

Rows 16 & 17: Dec 1 sc at beg, sc across (5 sc at end of last row).

Rows 18 & 19: Sc across.

Rows 20 through 22: Sc to last 2 sc, dec 1 sc (2 sc at end of last row).

Row 23: Sc in 2 sc, turn.

Row 24: Sk first sc, sl st in 2nd sc. Fasten off.

With stem stitch, embroider ear line and eye line on head section. With double strand, embroider nose on section. Sew head in place on motif, leaving lower edge of ear free. Embroider haunch line on motif.

Tail Pompon
Wind yarn 60 times around 2 fingers. Tie strands in center with a length of yarn, then cut loops open. Trim to 1½-inch shape. Sew tail in place.

TO FINISH
Sew motifs according to diagram.

Border

Rnd 1: From right side, join C in *back lp only* of a corner sp, sc, ch 1, and sc in same place for corner, * ch 1, sk 1 st, sc in *back lp only* of next st; rep from * evenly across edge to next corner. End with ch 1, sc, ch 1, and sc in *back lp only* of corner st. Continue in this way around entire outer edge. End with ch 1, join to first sc.

Rnds 2 through 8: Sl st to corner ch sp, ch 1, sc, and ch 1. Sc in same sp, * ch 1, sc in next ch sp; rep from * to next corner, end ch 1, in corner ch work sc, ch 1, and sc. Continue around and join. At end of last rnd, fasten off.

Edging

Rnd 1: Join A in a corner ch sp, ch 4, (dc in same sp, ch 1) 3 times, dc in same sp, sk 1 sc, sc in next sc, in next sc work dc, ch 1, dc, ch 1, dc (shell made), * sk 1 ch and 1 sc, sc in next ch sp, sk 1 sc and 1 ch, shell in next sc. Rep from * to corner ch sp, in sp work (dc, ch 1) 4 times, dc in same sp (corner shell made). Continue in this way around entire outer edge, join to 3rd ch at beg. Change to D.

Rnd 2: Sc in first sp of corner shell, ch 1, sc in next sp, ch 2, sc in next sp, ch 1, sc in next sp, ch 1, * sl st in sc, ch 1, sc in next sp, ch 2, sc in next sp, ch 1. Rep from * to corner shell, sc in first sp, ch 1, sc in next sp, ch 2, sc in next sp, ch 1, sc in next sp, ch 1. Continue around, join. Fasten off.

Inner Edging

Rnd 1: Join D in *front lp only* of a corner st of a corner motif, ch 3, dc, ch 1, and dc in same sp, * sk 1 st, sc in *front lp only* of next st, sk 1 st, shell as for edging in *front lp only* of next st. Rep from * to corner, work a corner shell with 4 dc in *front lp* of corner st, and continue around. Join to 2nd ch at beg. Change to A.

Rnd 2: Work same as Rnd 2 of edging.

VARIATION NO. 1
A – white
B – pink
C and D – gray

VARIATION NO. 2
A – white
B – pale blue
C and D – gray

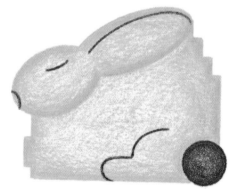

SLEEPING BUNNIES CHART

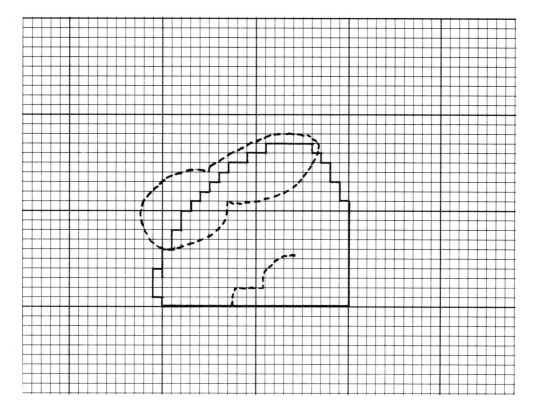

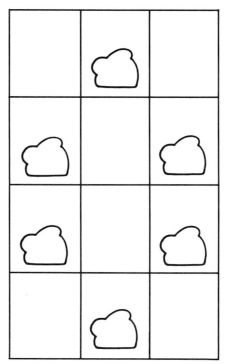

SLEEPING BUNNIES DIAGRAM

Victorian Rose

*T*here is nothing quite as lovely as an overall rose pattern on a white background. This project makes a very special wedding gift to treasure for many years and one that will be passed on to future generations. It is made with sport weight yarn and the finished size is 40 × 58 inches. A cross-stitch is used over the afghan stitch to create the designs.

MATERIALS: Bernat Berella Sportspun (1.75 oz./50 gram balls)—16 balls of MC (natural); 1 ball 2nd Edging color, CC (burgundy). **Embroidery Yarn:** DMC Floralia 3-ply Persian wool (5.4 yd. skeins)—9 each of A (yellow green) and B (medium forest green); 8 each of C (light yellow green) and D (dark rose); 7 of E (medium rose); 6 each of F (dusty rose) and G (pale pink); 3 of H (burgundy).

Afghan Hook: #8/H (5 mm) or size needed for correct gauge. Tapestry needle. Quickpoint needle.

GAUGE: 9 afghan sts = 2 inches; 4 rows = 1 inch.

DIRECTIONS

Refer to page 31 for complete afghan-stitch directions.

Strip (Make 3.)

Using the afghan hook and MC, ch 52 sts. Work even in afghan st for 227 rows. Sl st in each upright bar across last row. Break off MC. The piece should measure approximately 57 inches.

To Cross-Stitch Design on Afghan Stitch

Starting at the lower edge of the strip and using the tapestry needle and 2 strands of Floralia, work design in cross-stitch by following the chart. (See page 33 for cross-stitch details).

TO FINISH

First Edging: To be worked along left long edge of center strip and left long edge of right strip. With right side facing you and starting at left upper edge, work as follows:

Row 1: Using crochet hook, join MC in side of first row, ch 1, 1 sc in same row, * ch 3, skip next 2 rows, 1 sc in side of next row, repeat from *, ending last repeat, sk next 3 rows, 1 sc in side of last row.

Row 2: Ch 4 and turn. * 1 sc in next ch-3 sp, ch 3 *, repeat bet *s, ending 1 sc in last ch-3 sp, 1 sc in last st.

Row 3: Ch 4 and turn. Repeat bet *s of Row 2, ending 1 sc in 3rd st of turning ch.

Rows 4 & 5: Repeat Row 3. Fasten off.

Second Edging: To be worked along right long edge of center strip and right long edge of left strip. With right side facing you, starting at right lower edge, work in same manner as for Row 1 of First Edging. Fasten off.

To Join

Center and Left Strips: With right sides facing you, using crochet hook, join MC in ch sp at top of center strip, sl st in same sp, sl st in first st of left strip, 1 sc in first ch-3 sp of center strip, ch 1; insert hook under first ch-3 sp of left strip, yo hook and draw up a loop, yo and pull through 2 loops on hook (reverse sc); * ch 1, 1 sc in next ch-3 sp of center strip, ch 1, 1 reverse sc in next ch-3 sp of left strip.

Repeat from *, ending ch 1, sl st in last st of center strip, sl st in last st of left strip. Fasten off.

Right and Center Strips: With right sides facing you, using crochet hook, join MC in ch st at top of right strip and join in same manner as center and left strips.

Outer Edging

Rnd 1: With wrong side facing you, using crochet hook, join MC in any st and work in sc around entire afghan, working 3 sc in each corner.

Rnd 2: Ch 1, turn, 1 sc in each st around, working 3 sc in each corner st *and at the same time,* drop MC, draw CC through last 2 lps of last sc worked. *Do not turn.*

Rnd 3: Working from *left to right,* work 1 sc in each st around, join, and fasten off.

To Weave CC through First and Second Edgings

Cut 24 strands of CC 94 inches long. Thread Quickpoint needle with 6 strands. With right side of afghan facing you, start at one short end and work in 3rd and 4th rows of ch sps, leaving a 4-inch end. Bring the needle from *back to front* of work through 1st ch sp on 3rd row, insert needle from *front to back* into 1st ch sp on 4th row, * bring needle from *back to front* of work through next ch sp on 3rd row, insert needle from *front to back* into next ch sp on 4th row. Repeat from * to other short end, being careful not to pull yarn too tight. Break off yarn, leaving a 4-inch end. Secure ends on wrong side of work. Weave yarn in same manner on 5th and 6th rows of ch sps.

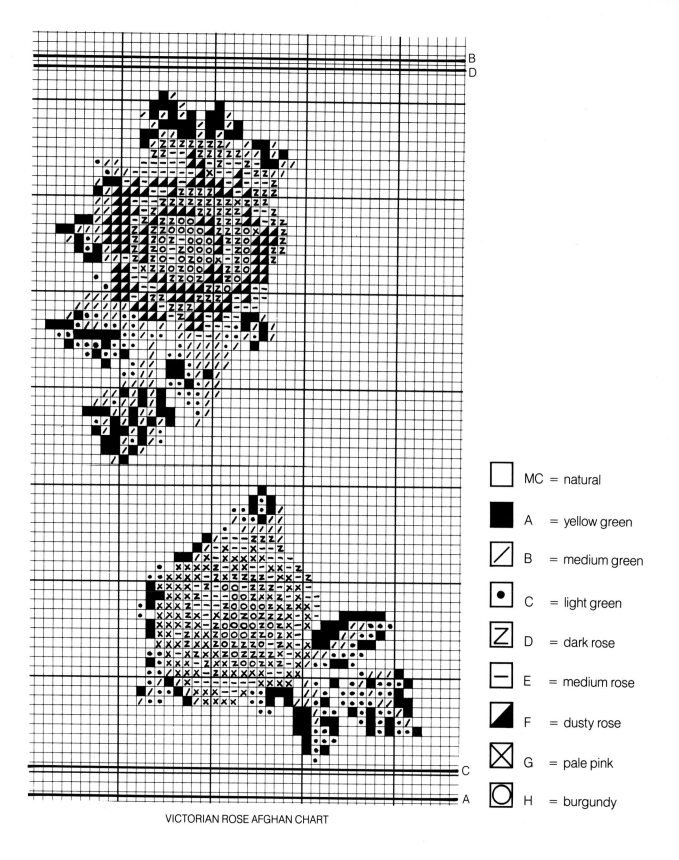

VICTORIAN ROSE AFGHAN CHART

MC = natural

A = yellow green

B = medium green

C = light green

D = dark rose

E = medium rose

F = dusty rose

G = pale pink

H = burgundy

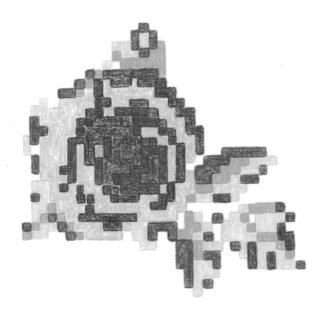

VARIATION NO. 1

MC – natural
A – yellow green
B – medium green
C – light green
D and H – dark fuchsia
E – light fuchsia
F and G – pale pink

VARIATION NO. 2

MC – natural
A – yellow green
B – medium green
C – light green
D and H – ochre
E – yellow orange
F and G – yellow

SAMPLER KNIT

A sampler afghan is always interesting and a project for the experienced knitter. When done in one color, such as ivory, the stitches and texture show off to their greatest advantage. This is a very elegant knit afghan measuring 50 × 60 inches.

MATERIALS: Unger's Utopia 4-ply acrylic (3.5 oz./100 gram balls)— 10 balls off-white.

Knitting Needles: #9 (5.5 mm) or size needed for correct gauge.

Crochet Hook: #9/I (5.5 mm).
Stitch markers.

GAUGE: Stockinette st: 4 sts = 1 inch; 6 rows = 1 inch. Each motif measures 10 × 12 inches.

DIRECTIONS

Diamond Motif (Make 13.)

Cast on 41 sts. Work 5 rows in garter st (k each row). Beg pat.

Row 1 (right side): K 4 for garter-st border; place marker, k 4, * p 1, k 7. Rep from * to last 9 sts, p 1, k 4, place marker, k 4 for garter-st border.

Row 2: K 4 for border; p 3, * k 1, p 1, k 1, p 5. Rep from * to last 10 sts, k 1, p 1, k 1, p 3, k 4 for border.

Row 3: K 4 for border; k 2, * p 1, k 3. Rep from * to last 7 sts, p 1, k 2; k 4 for border.

Row 4: K 4; p 1, k 1, * p 5, k 1, p 1, k 1. Rep from * to last 11 sts, p 5, k 1, p 1; k 4.

Row 5: K 4; * p 1, k 7. Rep from * to last 5 sts, p 1; k 4.

Row 6: Rep Row 4.

Row 7: Rep Row 3.

Row 8: Rep Row 2.
Rep Rows 1 through 8 seven times; then rep Row 1 once more. Work in garter st on all sts for 4 rows. Bind off.

Cob Stitch Motif (Make 12.)

Cast on 39 sts. Work 5 rows in garter st. Beg pat.

Row 1 (right side): K 4 for garter-st border; place marker, p 3, * in next st work k 1, yo, k 1—cob st (CS) made. P 3. Rep from * to last 4 sts, place marker; k 4 for garter-st border.

Row 2: K 4 for border; k 3, * p 3, k 3. Rep from * to last 4 sts; k 4.

Row 3: K 4; p 3, * k 3, p 3. Rep from * to last 4 sts; k 4.

Row 4: K 4 for border; k 3, * p 3 tog, k 3. Rep from * to last 4 sts; k 4.

Row 5: K 4, p to last 4 sts; k 4.

Row 6: K all sts.

Row 7: K 4; p 1, * CS, p 3. Rep from * to last 6 sts; CS, p 1; k 4.

Row 8: K 4 for border; k 1, * p 3, k 3. Rep from * to last 8 sts, p 3, k 1; k 4 for border.

Row 9: K 4; p 1, * k 3, p 3. Rep from * to last 8 sts, k 3, p 1; k 4.

Row 10: K 4 for border; k 1, * p 3 tog, k 3. Rep from * to last 8 sts, p 3 tog, k 1; k 4 for border.

Row 11: Rep Row 5.

Row 12: Rep Row 6.
Rep Rows 1 through 12 for pat 4 times, then rep Rows 1 through 4 once. Work in garter st on all sts for 4 rows. Bind off.

TO FINISH

Sew motifs tog, alternating diamond and cob-st motifs so you have 5 rows of 5 motifs in each. From right side with hook, sc evenly across each narrow edge.

Fringe: Fold five 21-inch strands in half and knot across upper and lower edges. Place about 3 in each motif and 1 in each motif edge. Divide lengths of each fringe and knot with adjacent fringe 1¼ inch below; then divide fringe again and knot 1¼ inch below first row of knots. Trim all fringe evenly.

Peachy Crib Cover

*I*t's fun to make a baby blanket. The project is always appreciated by the new parents, and the gift is both good-looking and useful. If you're expecting a new arrival, this is the perfect carry-along project to work on while waiting in the doctor's office and during other waiting or leisure time. The squares that make up the afghan are 5 inches.

Made of 100% acrylic, the afghan is completely washable. While I chose peach color for the entire project, you might prefer combining several colors or using a two-color combination. Almost any color will go well with white, so choose a bright, bold primary color or a soft color combination. This crochet pattern is quite versatile. The finished afghan is 40 × 52 inches.

MATERIALS: Caron International acrylic yarn (3 oz./75 gram balls)—6 skeins peach.

Crochet Hook: #6/G (4.5 mm)

GAUGE: 1 motif = 5 × 5 inches.

DIRECTIONS

Make 48 squares.

Begin with ch 7, sl st in first ch to form ring.

Rnd 1: Ch 2 (counts as 1 dc), 2 dc in ring, ch 3. (3 dc in ring, ch 3) 3 times; sl st in top of ch 2 at beg of rnd.

Rnd 2: Ch 2, dc in each of next 2 dc, 2 dc, ch 3, 2 dc in corner sp, (dc in each of next 3 dc, 2 dc, ch 3, 2 dc in corner sp) 3 times; sl st in top of ch 2.

Rnd 3: Ch 2, dc in each of next 4 dc, 2 dc, ch 3, 2 dc in corner sp, (dc in each of next 7 dc, 2 dc, ch 3, 2 dc in corner sp) 3 times; dc in last 2 dc, sl st in top of ch 2.

Rnd 4: Ch 2, dc in each of next 6 dc, 2 dc, ch 3, 2 dc in corner sp, (dc in each of next 15 dc, 2 dc, ch 3, 2 dc in corner sp) 3 times; dc in last 6 dc, sl st in top of ch 2.

Rnd 6: Ch 2, dc in each of next 10 dc, 2 dc, ch 3, 2 dc in corner sp, (dc in each of next 19 dc, 2 dc, ch 3, 2 dc in corner sp) 3 times; dc in last 8 dc, sl st in top of ch 2. Fasten off.

TO FINISH

Arrange squares in rows of 6 across and 8 down. Sc squares tog from wrong side, working 1 sc through *back loops only* of each pair of corresponding dc and working 1 sc in corner sps.

Picot Edging

Attach yarn at any corner. *Sc in next 6 sts, ch 2, sc in last st; rep around from *.

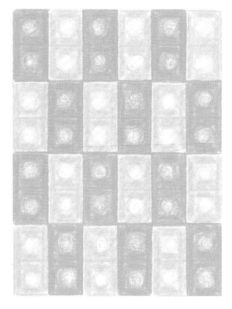

VARIATION NO. 1

Use equal amounts of aqua and yellow. Follow color sketch for assembly of squares.

VARIATION NO. 2

Use equal amounts of pink and white. Follow color sketch for assembly of squares.

Bright Knit

*T*he beautiful deep pinks and purples of this knit afghan are set off by the dark frames. This is quite reminiscent of quilt patterns with patchwork blocks and lattices. While this afghan is made in vibrant colors, you might select a combination of Caribbean or ice cream colors for a totally different project.

The finished size is 67 inches square, which makes it perfect as a lap throw in the living room, bedroom, or den. The bright colors would please any child.

MATERIALS: Phildar's Pegase knitting worsted (1.75 oz./50 gram skeins)—8 balls each of A (light blue), C (deep blue), D (deep rose), E (purple); Prognostic knitting worsted (1.75 oz./50 gram skeins)—23 skeins of B (black or navy blue).

Knitting Needles: #9 (5.5 mm) or size needed for correct gauge.

Crochet Hook: #6/G (4.5 mm).

GAUGE: Use double strand of Pegase or triple strand of Prognostic throughout. Stockinette st: 14 sts = 4 inches; 20 rows = 4 inches.

Ribbed sc: In sc, insert crochet hook under the *back loop* of the stitch from previous row.

DIRECTIONS

Use double strand of Pegase or triple strand of Prognostic throughout. This afghan is made in strips and then joined with the crochet hook. There are 5 narrow strips and 4 wide strips.

Narrow Strip (Make 5.)
With color A, cast on 14 sts (double strand) and work in stockinette (St) st (1 row knit, next row purl) as follows:
16 rows A (double strand).
58 rows B (triple strand).
16 rows C (double strand).
58 rows B (triple strand).
16 rows A (double strand).
58 rows B (triple strand).
16 rows D (double strand).
58 rows B (triple strand).
16 rows C (double strand).
Bind off. Make 4 more strips following the color sequence shown on the chart.

Wide Strip (Make 4.)
With color B (triple strand), cast on 44 sts and work in St st as follows:
16 rows B (triple strand).
58 rows D (double strand).
16 rows B (triple strand).
58 rows E (double strand).
16 rows B (triple strand).
58 rows A (double strand).
16 rows B (triple strand).
58 rows E (double strand).
16 rows B (triple strand).
Bind off. Make 3 more strips following the color sequence as shown on the chart.

TO FINISH

Block every strip on the wrong side with a damp cloth and press with a warm iron. Sew strips together as shown in the chart. With the crochet hook and color B (triple strand), make 1 row in sc, then 4 rows in ribbed sc around blanket.

Original Color Scheme

C	B	A	B	D	B	E	B	A
B	E	B	C	B	A	B	D	B
D	B	D	B	E	B	C	B	E
B	A	B	D	B	E	B	C	B
A	B	C	B	A	B	E	B	D
B	E	B	C	B	D	B	A	B
C	B	E	B	A	B	C	B	C
B	D	B	A	B	C	B	E	B
A	B	C	B	E	B	A	B	D

A – light blue
B – navy blue
C – deep blue
D – deep rose
E – purple

BRIGHT KNIT CHARTS

A	B	C	B	D	B	E	B	A
B	D	B	A	B	E	B	C	B
C	B	E	B	D	B	D	B	E
B	E	B	C	B	A	B	E	B
C	B	D	B	A	B	C	B	C
B	A		E	B	A	B	C	B
E	B	C	B	A	B	A	B	D
B	D	B	A	B	C	B	E	B
A	B	E	B	C	B	D	B	A

A – aqua
B – lavender
C – lime
D – lemon
E – rose

A	B	E	B	D	B	D	B	A
B	C	B	A	B	E	B	C	B
E	B	D	B	C	B	E	B	D
B	A	B	C	B	D	B	A	B
D	B	A	B	A	B	C	B	C
B	D	B	C	B	A	B	E	B
C	B	A	B	E	B	C	B	E
B	E	B	D	B	E	B	D	B
A	B	E	B	D	B	E	B	A

A – dark brown
B – grey
C – tan
D – sienna
E – clay red

VARIATION NO. 1

A – dark brown
B – gray
C – tan
D – sienna
E – clay red

VARIATION NO. 2

A – aqua
B – lavender
C – lime
D – lemon
E – rose

Index

All of us at Sedgewood® Press are dedicated to offering you, our customer, the best books we can create. We are particularly concerned that all of the instructions for making the projects are clear and accurate. We welcome your comments and would like to hear any suggestions you may have. Please address your correspondence to Customer Service Department, Sedgewood® Press, Meredith Corporation, 750 Third Avenue, New York, NY 10017.

For information on how you can have *Better Homes and Gardens* delivered to your door, write to: Mr. Robert Austin, P.O. Box 4536, Des Moines, IA 50336.